Garden J

Name:

PLANT TYPE AND VARIETY	DATE PLANTED	TODAY'S DATE

How tall is your plant?

_____

How many leaves does it have?

_____

Do you see any bug on or near your plant?

_____

If so, what do they look like and what are they doing?

_____

_____

Describe interesting observations about your plant.

_____

_____

_____

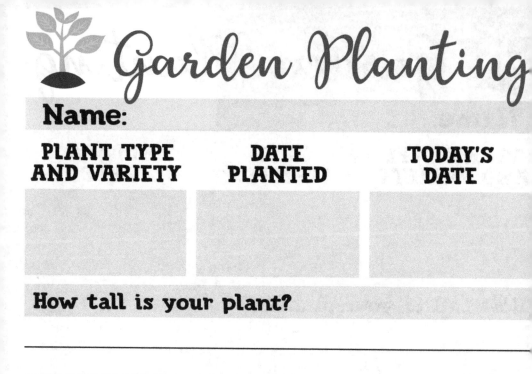

Garden Planting

Name:

PLANT TYPE AND VARIETY	DATE PLANTED	TODAY'S DATE

How tall is your plant?

_____

How many leaves does it have?

_____

Do you see any bug on or near your plant?

_____

If so. what do they look like and what are they doing?

_____

_____

Describe interesting observations about your plant.

_____

_____

_____

Garden Planting

Name:

PLANT TYPE AND VARIETY	DATE PLANTED	TODAY'S DATE

How tall is your plant?

_____

How many leaves does it have?

_____

Do you see any bug on or near your plant?

_____

If so. what do they look like and what are they doing?

_____

_____

Describe interesting observations about your plant.

_____

_____

_____

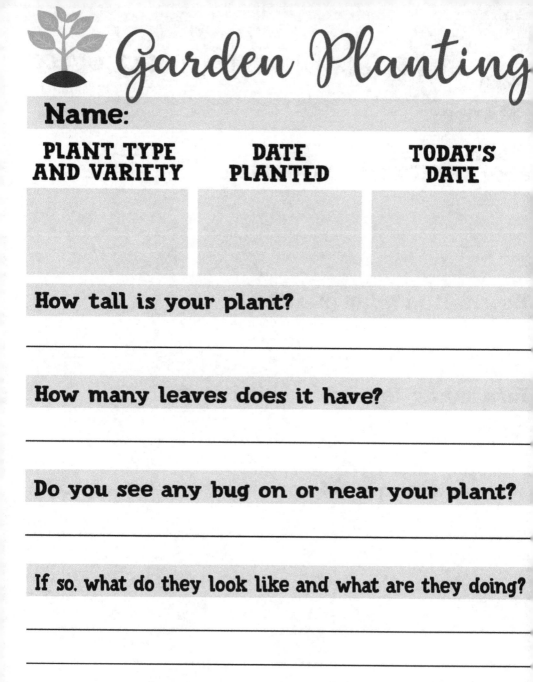

Garden Planting

Name:

PLANT TYPE AND VARIETY	DATE PLANTED	TODAY'S DATE

How tall is your plant?

_____

How many leaves does it have?

_____

Do you see any bug on or near your plant?

_____

If so, what do they look like and what are they doing?

_____

_____

Describe interesting observations about your plant.

_____

_____

_____

Garden Planting

Name:

PLANT TYPE AND VARIETY	DATE PLANTED	TODAY'S DATE

How tall is your plant?

_____

How many leaves does it have?

_____

Do you see any bug on or near your plant?

_____

If so. what do they look like and what are they doing?

_____

_____

Describe interesting observations about your plant.

_____

_____

_____

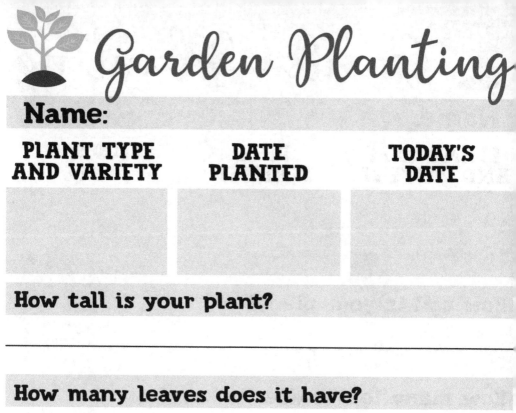

Garden Planting

Name:

PLANT TYPE AND VARIETY	DATE PLANTED	TODAY'S DATE

How tall is your plant?

_____

How many leaves does it have?

_____

Do you see any bug on or near your plant?

_____

If so. what do they look like and what are they doing?

_____

_____

Describe interesting observations about your plant.

_____

_____

_____

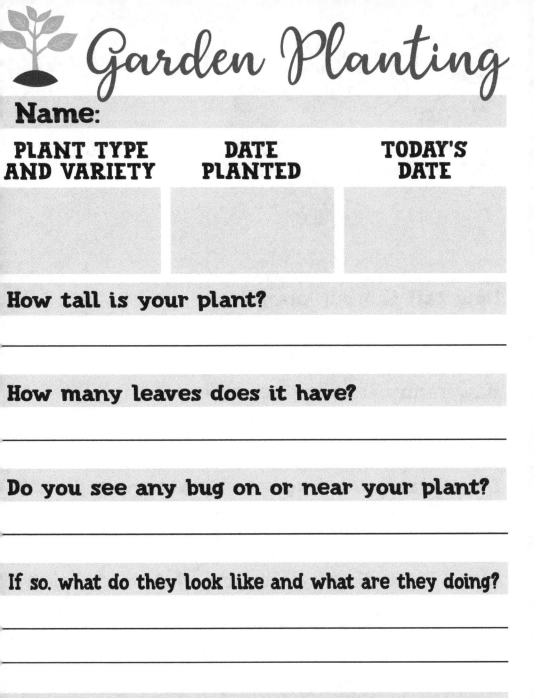

Garden Planting

Name:

PLANT TYPE AND VARIETY	DATE PLANTED	TODAY'S DATE

How tall is your plant?

_____

How many leaves does it have?

_____

Do you see any bug on or near your plant?

_____

If so, what do they look like and what are they doing?

_____

_____

Describe interesting observations about your plant.

_____

_____

_____

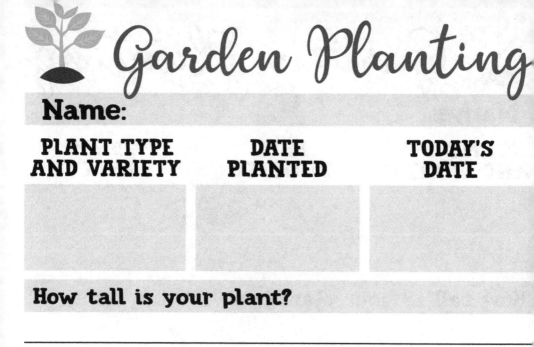

Garden Planting

Name:

PLANT TYPE AND VARIETY	DATE PLANTED	TODAY'S DATE

How tall is your plant?

_____

How many leaves does it have?

_____

Do you see any bug on or near your plant?

_____

If so, what do they look like and what are they doing?

_____

_____

Describe interesting observations about your plant.

_____

_____

_____

Garden Planting

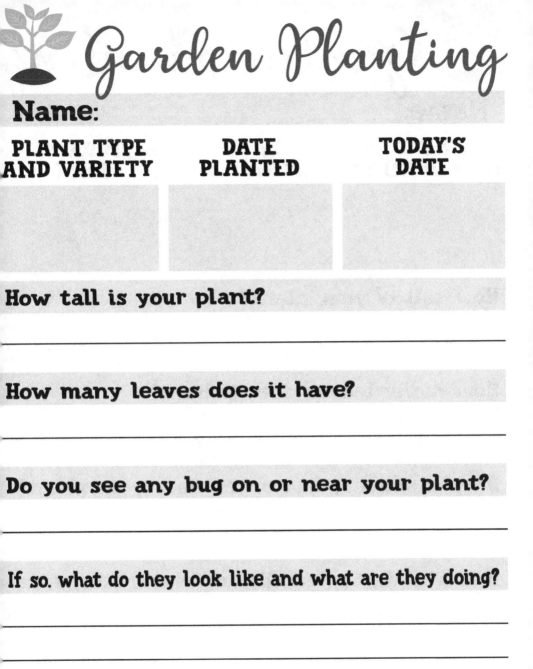

Name:

PLANT TYPE AND VARIETY	DATE PLANTED	TODAY'S DATE

How tall is your plant?

_____

How many leaves does it have?

_____

Do you see any bug on or near your plant?

_____

If so. what do they look like and what are they doing?

_____

_____

Describe interesting observations about your plant.

_____

_____

_____

Garden Planting

Name:

PLANT TYPE AND VARIETY	DATE PLANTED	TODAY'S DATE

How tall is your plant?

_____

How many leaves does it have?

_____

Do you see any bug on or near your plant?

_____

If so. what do they look like and what are they doing?

_____

_____

Describe interesting observations about your plant.

_____

_____

_____

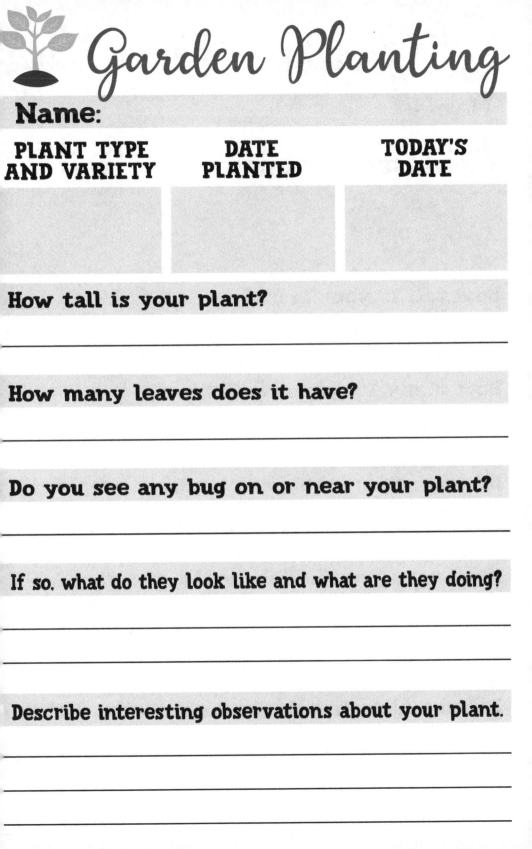

Garden Planting

Name:

PLANT TYPE AND VARIETY	DATE PLANTED	TODAY'S DATE

How tall is your plant?

_____

How many leaves does it have?

_____

Do you see any bug on or near your plant?

_____

If so, what do they look like and what are they doing?

_____

_____

Describe interesting observations about your plant.

_____

_____

_____

_____

Garden Planting

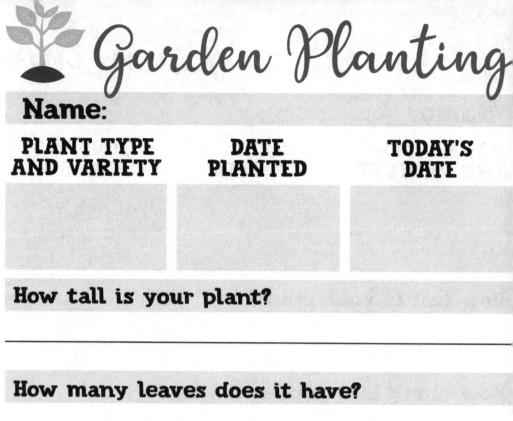

Name:

PLANT TYPE AND VARIETY	DATE PLANTED	TODAY'S DATE

How tall is your plant?

_____

How many leaves does it have?

_____

Do you see any bug on or near your plant?

_____

If so, what do they look like and what are they doing?

_____

_____

Describe interesting observations about your plant.

_____

_____

_____

Garden Planting

Name:

PLANT TYPE AND VARIETY	DATE PLANTED	TODAY'S DATE

How tall is your plant?

_____

How many leaves does it have?

_____

Do you see any bug on or near your plant?

_____

If so, what do they look like and what are they doing?

_____

_____

Describe interesting observations about your plant.

_____

_____

_____

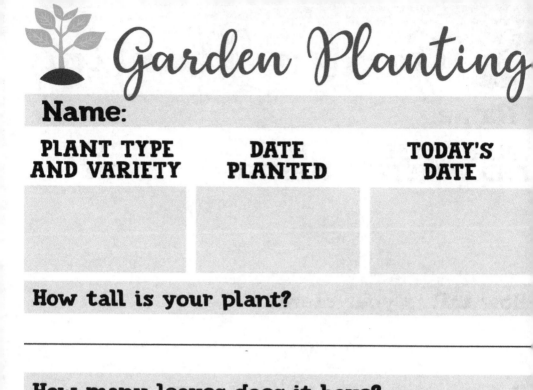

Garden Planting

Name:

PLANT TYPE AND VARIETY	DATE PLANTED	TODAY'S DATE

How tall is your plant?

_____

How many leaves does it have?

_____

Do you see any bug on or near your plant?

_____

If so, what do they look like and what are they doing?

_____

_____

Describe interesting observations about your plant.

_____

_____

_____

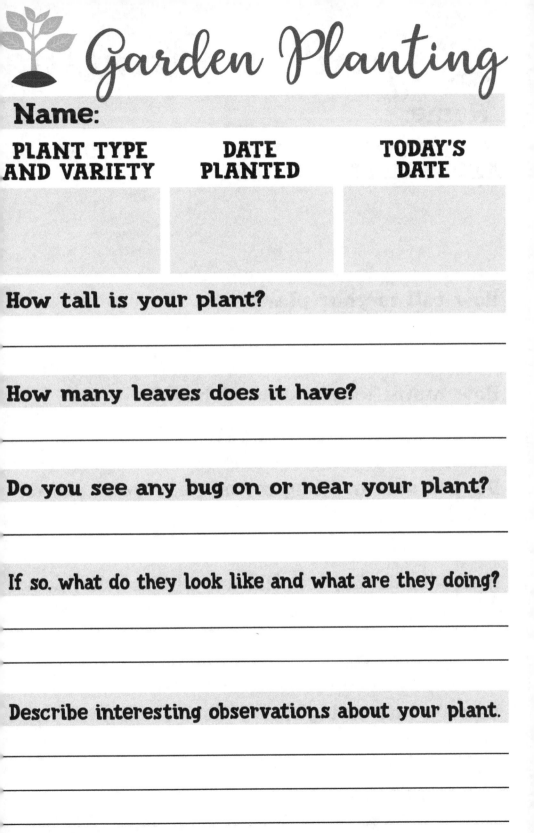

Garden Planting

Name:

PLANT TYPE AND VARIETY	DATE PLANTED	TODAY'S DATE

How tall is your plant?

_____

How many leaves does it have?

_____

Do you see any bug on or near your plant?

_____

If so. what do they look like and what are they doing?

_____

_____

Describe interesting observations about your plant.

_____

_____

_____

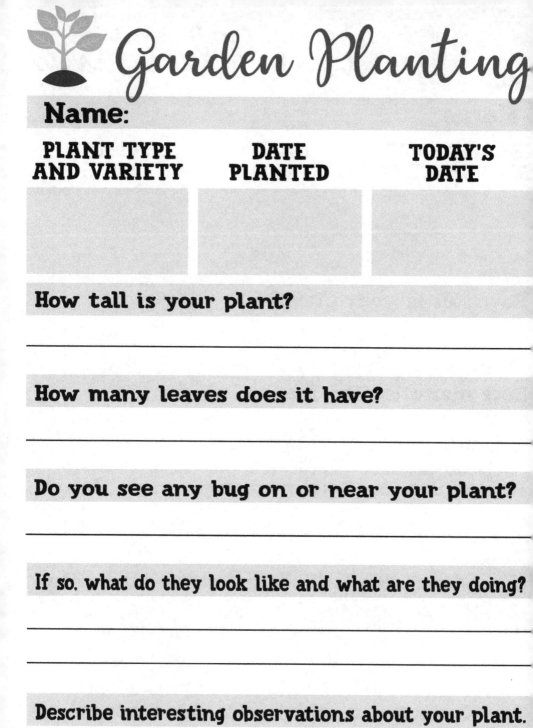

Garden Planting

Name:

PLANT TYPE AND VARIETY	DATE PLANTED	TODAY'S DATE

How tall is your plant?

_____

How many leaves does it have?

_____

Do you see any bug on or near your plant?

_____

If so, what do they look like and what are they doing?

_____

_____

Describe interesting observations about your plant.

_____

_____

_____

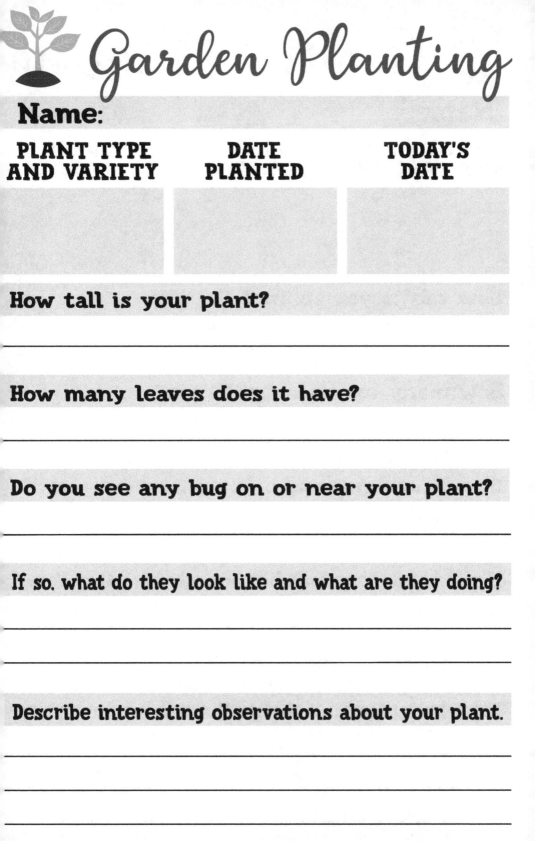

Garden Planting

Name:

PLANT TYPE AND VARIETY	DATE PLANTED	TODAY'S DATE

How tall is your plant?

_____

How many leaves does it have?

_____

Do you see any bug on or near your plant?

_____

If so, what do they look like and what are they doing?

_____

_____

Describe interesting observations about your plant.

_____

_____

_____

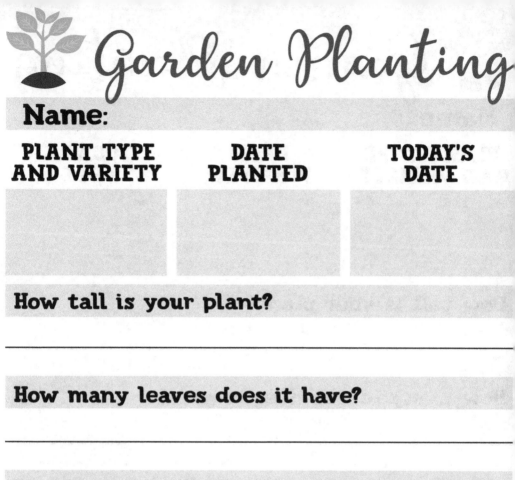

Garden Planting

Name:

PLANT TYPE AND VARIETY	DATE PLANTED	TODAY'S DATE

How tall is your plant?

_____

How many leaves does it have?

_____

Do you see any bug on or near your plant?

_____

If so, what do they look like and what are they doing?

_____

_____

Describe interesting observations about your plant.

_____

_____

_____

Garden Planting

Name:

PLANT TYPE AND VARIETY	DATE PLANTED	TODAY'S DATE

How tall is your plant?

_____

How many leaves does it have?

_____

Do you see any bug on or near your plant?

_____

If so. what do they look like and what are they doing?

_____

_____

Describe interesting observations about your plant.

_____

_____

_____

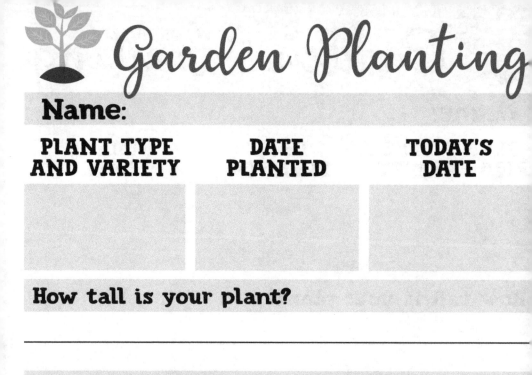

Garden Planting

Name:

PLANT TYPE AND VARIETY	DATE PLANTED	TODAY'S DATE

How tall is your plant?

_____

How many leaves does it have?

_____

Do you see any bug on or near your plant?

_____

If so. what do they look like and what are they doing?

_____

_____

Describe interesting observations about your plant.

_____

_____

_____

Garden Planting

Name:

PLANT TYPE AND VARIETY	DATE PLANTED	TODAY'S DATE

How tall is your plant?

_____

How many leaves does it have?

_____

Do you see any bug on or near your plant?

_____

If so. what do they look like and what are they doing?

_____

_____

Describe interesting observations about your plant.

_____

_____

_____

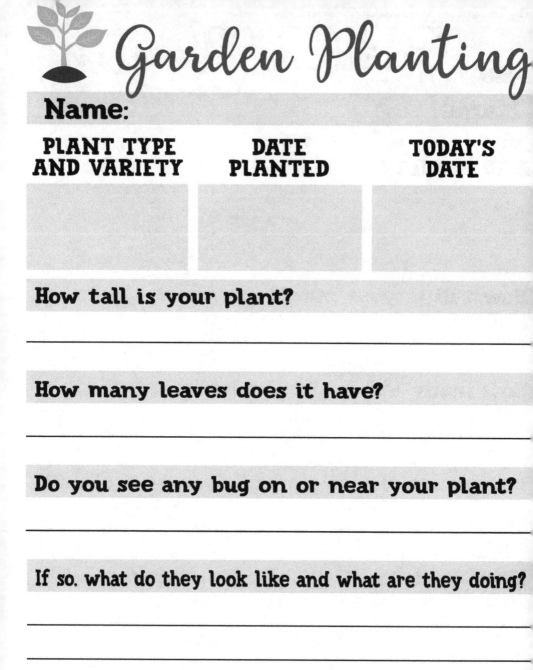

Garden Planting

Name:

PLANT TYPE AND VARIETY	DATE PLANTED	TODAY'S DATE

How tall is your plant?

_____

How many leaves does it have?

_____

Do you see any bug on or near your plant?

_____

If so, what do they look like and what are they doing?

_____

_____

Describe interesting observations about your plant.

_____

_____

_____

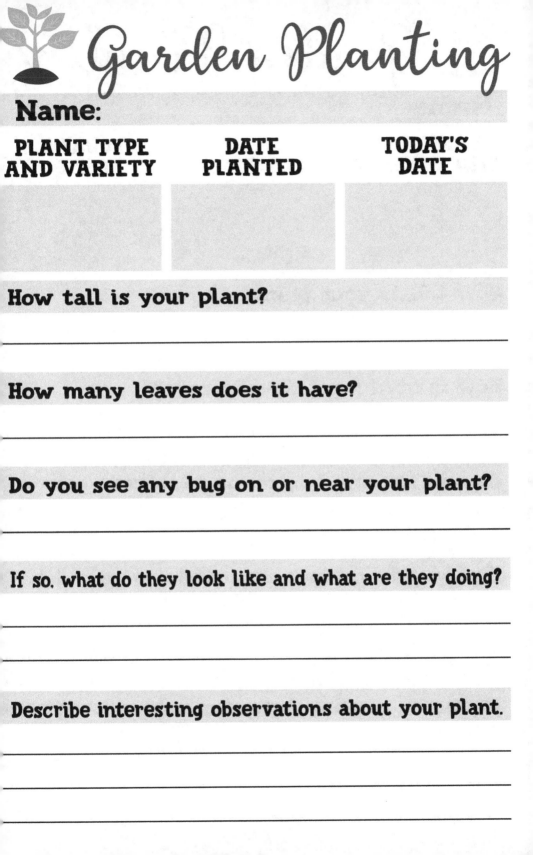

Garden Planting

Name:

PLANT TYPE AND VARIETY	DATE PLANTED	TODAY'S DATE

How tall is your plant?

_____

How many leaves does it have?

_____

Do you see any bug on or near your plant?

_____

If so. what do they look like and what are they doing?

_____

_____

Describe interesting observations about your plant.

_____

_____

_____

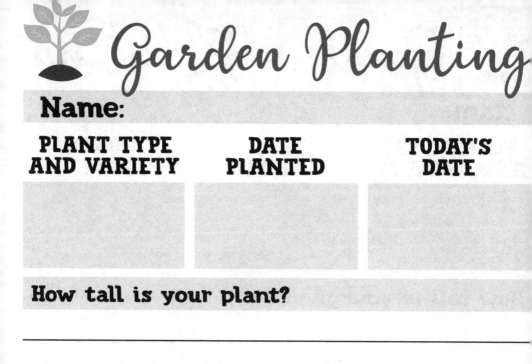

Garden Planting

Name:

PLANT TYPE AND VARIETY	DATE PLANTED	TODAY'S DATE

How tall is your plant?

_____

How many leaves does it have?

_____

Do you see any bug on or near your plant?

_____

If so, what do they look like and what are they doing?

_____

_____

Describe interesting observations about your plant.

_____

_____

_____

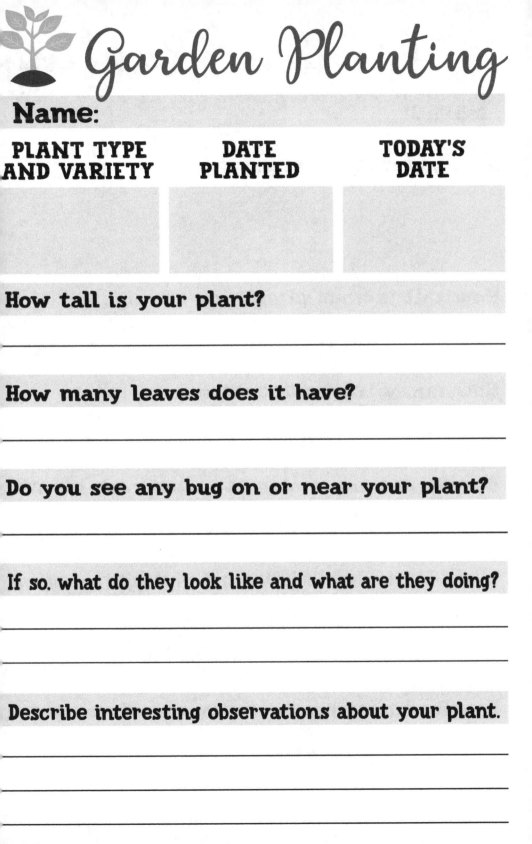

Garden Planting

Name:

PLANT TYPE AND VARIETY	DATE PLANTED	TODAY'S DATE

How tall is your plant?

_____

How many leaves does it have?

_____

Do you see any bug on or near your plant?

_____

If so. what do they look like and what are they doing?

_____

_____

Describe interesting observations about your plant.

_____

_____

_____

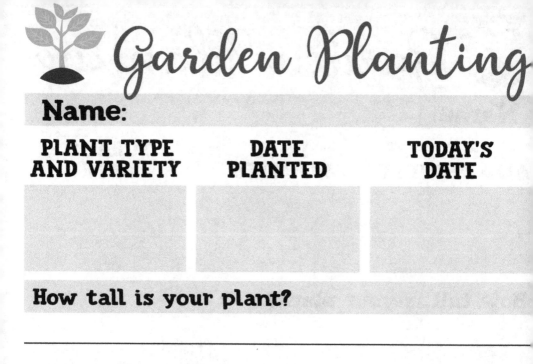

Garden Planting

Name:

PLANT TYPE AND VARIETY	DATE PLANTED	TODAY'S DATE

How tall is your plant?

_____

How many leaves does it have?

_____

Do you see any bug on or near your plant?

_____

If so. what do they look like and what are they doing?

_____

_____

Describe interesting observations about your plant.

_____

_____

_____

Garden Planting

Name:

PLANT TYPE AND VARIETY	DATE PLANTED	TODAY'S DATE

How tall is your plant?

_____

How many leaves does it have?

_____

Do you see any bug on or near your plant?

_____

If so. what do they look like and what are they doing?

_____

_____

Describe interesting observations about your plant.

_____

_____

_____

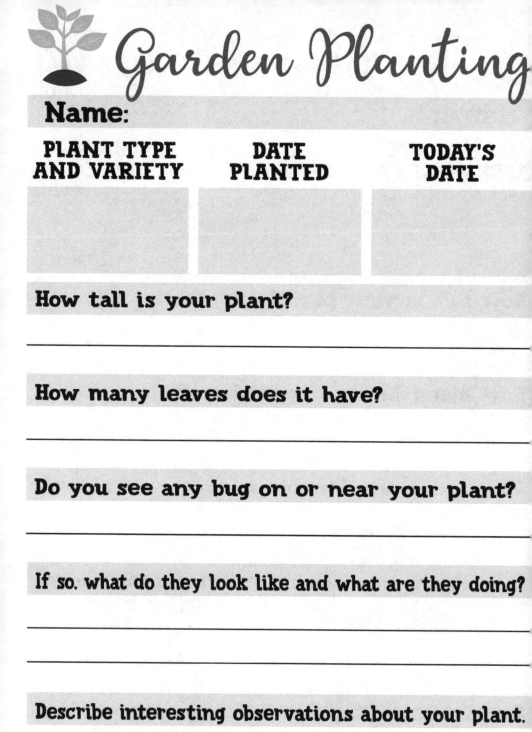

Garden Planting

Name:

PLANT TYPE AND VARIETY	DATE PLANTED	TODAY'S DATE

How tall is your plant?

_____

How many leaves does it have?

_____

Do you see any bug on or near your plant?

_____

If so, what do they look like and what are they doing?

_____

_____

Describe interesting observations about your plant.

_____

_____

_____

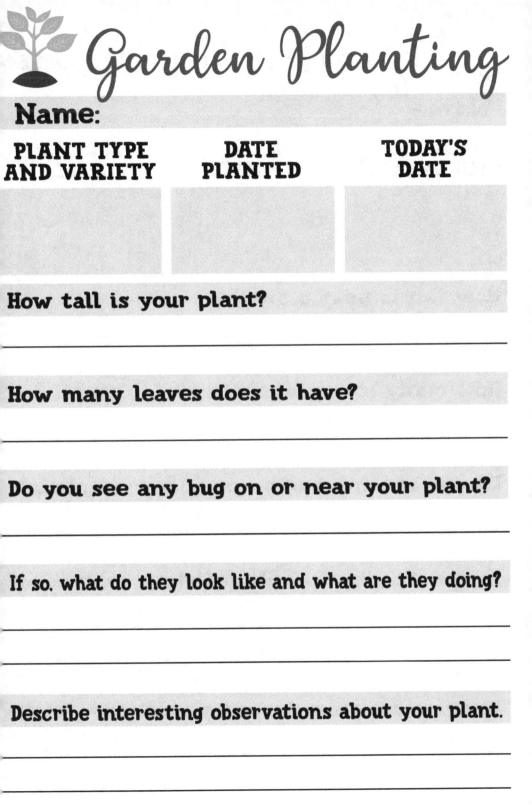

Garden Planting

Name:

PLANT TYPE AND VARIETY	DATE PLANTED	TODAY'S DATE

How tall is your plant?

_____

How many leaves does it have?

_____

Do you see any bug on or near your plant?

_____

If so, what do they look like and what are they doing?

_____

_____

Describe interesting observations about your plant.

_____

_____

_____

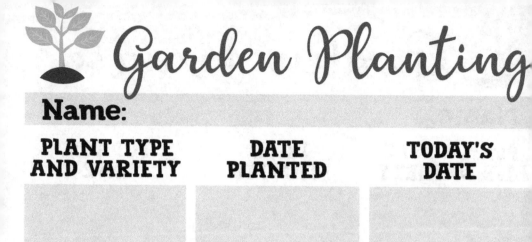

Garden Planting

Name:

PLANT TYPE AND VARIETY	DATE PLANTED	TODAY'S DATE

How tall is your plant?

_____

How many leaves does it have?

_____

Do you see any bug on or near your plant?

_____

If so, what do they look like and what are they doing?

_____

_____

Describe interesting observations about your plant.

_____

_____

_____

Garden Planting

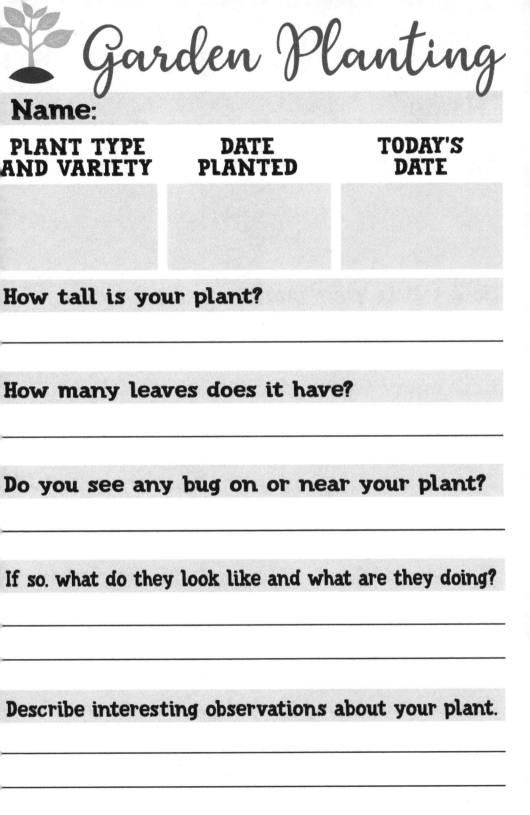

Name:

PLANT TYPE AND VARIETY	DATE PLANTED	TODAY'S DATE

How tall is your plant?

_____

How many leaves does it have?

_____

Do you see any bug on or near your plant?

_____

If so, what do they look like and what are they doing?

_____

_____

Describe interesting observations about your plant.

_____

_____

_____

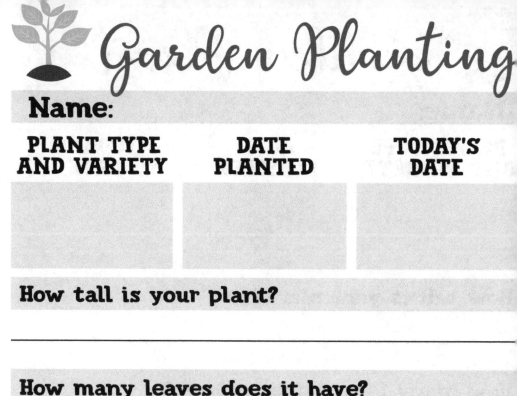

Garden Planting

Name:

PLANT TYPE AND VARIETY	DATE PLANTED	TODAY'S DATE

How tall is your plant?

_____

How many leaves does it have?

_____

Do you see any bug on or near your plant?

_____

If so. what do they look like and what are they doing?

_____

_____

Describe interesting observations about your plant.

_____

_____

_____

Garden Planting

Name:

PLANT TYPE AND VARIETY	DATE PLANTED	TODAY'S DATE

How tall is your plant?

How many leaves does it have?

Do you see any bug on or near your plant?

If so. what do they look like and what are they doing?

Describe interesting observations about your plant.

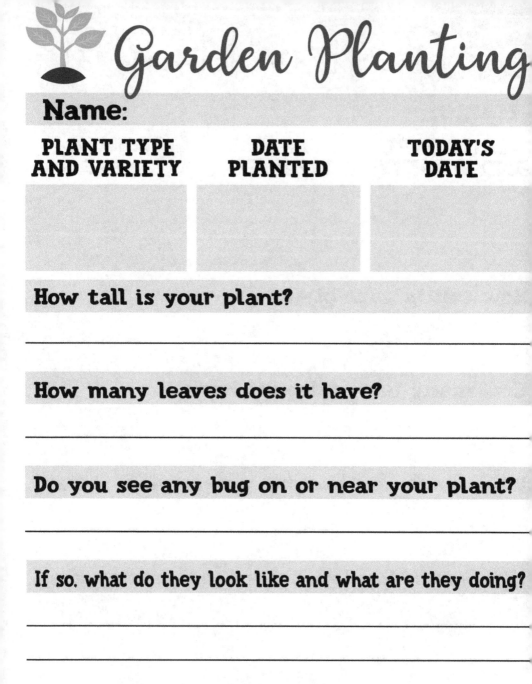

Garden Planting

Name:

PLANT TYPE AND VARIETY	DATE PLANTED	TODAY'S DATE

How tall is your plant?

_____

How many leaves does it have?

_____

Do you see any bug on or near your plant?

_____

If so. what do they look like and what are they doing?

_____

_____

Describe interesting observations about your plant.

_____

_____

_____

Garden Planting

Name:

PLANT TYPE AND VARIETY	DATE PLANTED	TODAY'S DATE

How tall is your plant?

_____

How many leaves does it have?

_____

Do you see any bug on or near your plant?

_____

If so. what do they look like and what are they doing?

_____

_____

Describe interesting observations about your plant.

_____

_____

_____

Garden Planting

Name:

PLANT TYPE AND VARIETY	DATE PLANTED	TODAY'S DATE

How tall is your plant?

_____

How many leaves does it have?

_____

Do you see any bug on or near your plant?

_____

If so. what do they look like and what are they doing?

_____

_____

Describe interesting observations about your plant.

_____

_____

_____

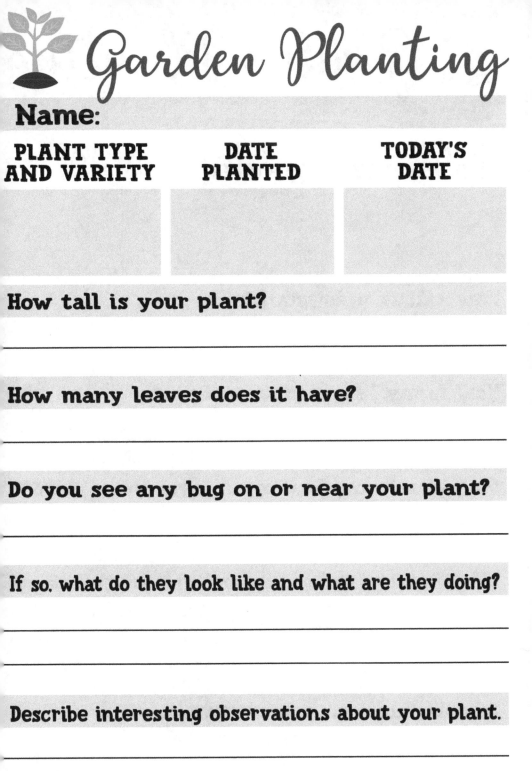

Garden Planting

Name:

PLANT TYPE AND VARIETY	DATE PLANTED	TODAY'S DATE

How tall is your plant?

_____

How many leaves does it have?

_____

Do you see any bug on or near your plant?

_____

If so. what do they look like and what are they doing?

_____

_____

Describe interesting observations about your plant.

_____

_____

_____

_____

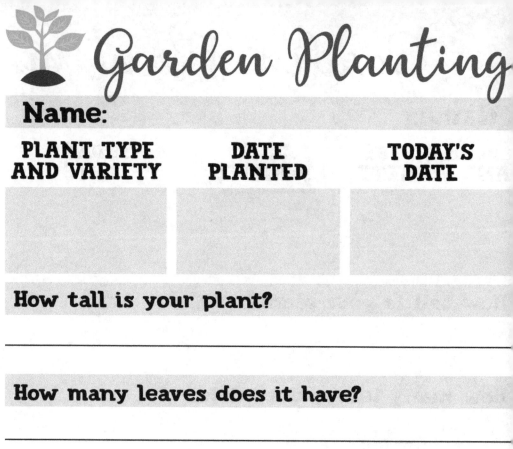

Garden Planting

Name:

PLANT TYPE AND VARIETY	DATE PLANTED	TODAY'S DATE

How tall is your plant?

_____

How many leaves does it have?

_____

Do you see any bug on or near your plant?

_____

If so. what do they look like and what are they doing?

_____

_____

Describe interesting observations about your plant.

_____

_____

_____

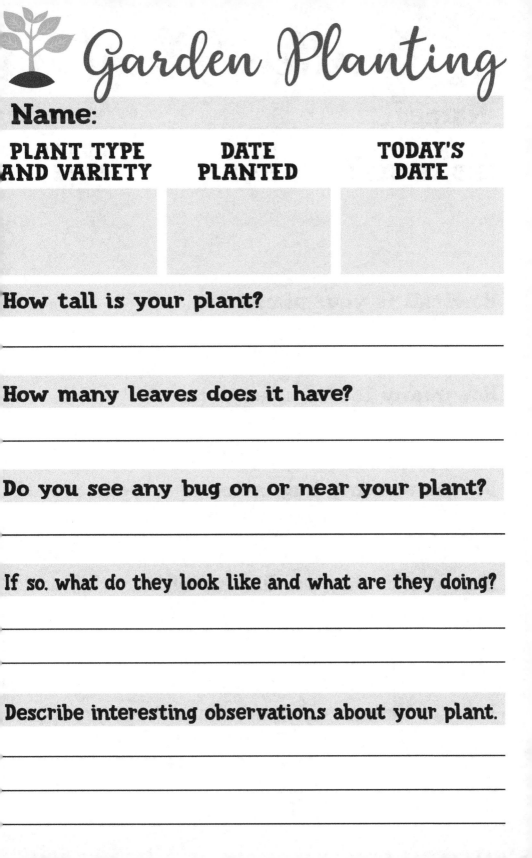

Garden Planting

Name:

PLANT TYPE AND VARIETY	DATE PLANTED	TODAY'S DATE

How tall is your plant?

_____

How many leaves does it have?

_____

Do you see any bug on or near your plant?

_____

If so. what do they look like and what are they doing?

_____

_____

Describe interesting observations about your plant.

_____

_____

_____

Garden Planting

Name:

PLANT TYPE AND VARIETY	DATE PLANTED	TODAY'S DATE

How tall is your plant?

_____

How many leaves does it have?

_____

Do you see any bug on or near your plant?

_____

If so, what do they look like and what are they doing?

_____

_____

Describe interesting observations about your plant.

_____

_____

_____

Garden Planting

Name:

PLANT TYPE AND VARIETY	DATE PLANTED	TODAY'S DATE

How tall is your plant?

_____

How many leaves does it have?

_____

Do you see any bug on or near your plant?

_____

If so, what do they look like and what are they doing?

_____

_____

Describe interesting observations about your plant.

_____

_____

_____

_____

Garden Planting

Name:

PLANT TYPE AND VARIETY	DATE PLANTED	TODAY'S DATE

How tall is your plant?

_____

How many leaves does it have?

_____

Do you see any bug on or near your plant?

_____

If so. what do they look like and what are they doing?

_____

_____

Describe interesting observations about your plant.

_____

_____

_____

Garden Planting

Name:

PLANT TYPE AND VARIETY	DATE PLANTED	TODAY'S DATE

How tall is your plant?

_____

How many leaves does it have?

_____

Do you see any bug on or near your plant?

_____

If so. what do they look like and what are they doing?

_____

_____

Describe interesting observations about your plant.

_____

_____

_____

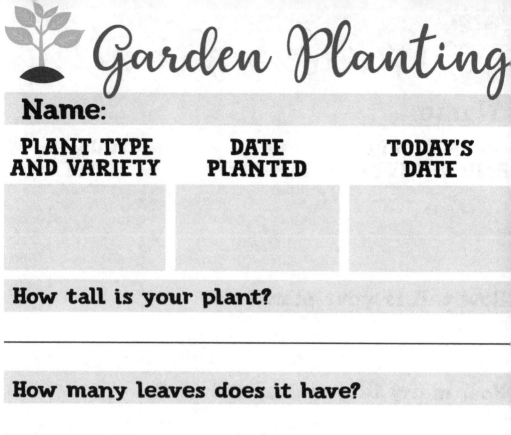

Garden Planting

Name:

PLANT TYPE AND VARIETY	DATE PLANTED	TODAY'S DATE

How tall is your plant?

_____

How many leaves does it have?

_____

Do you see any bug on or near your plant?

_____

If so, what do they look like and what are they doing?

_____

_____

Describe interesting observations about your plant.

_____

_____

_____

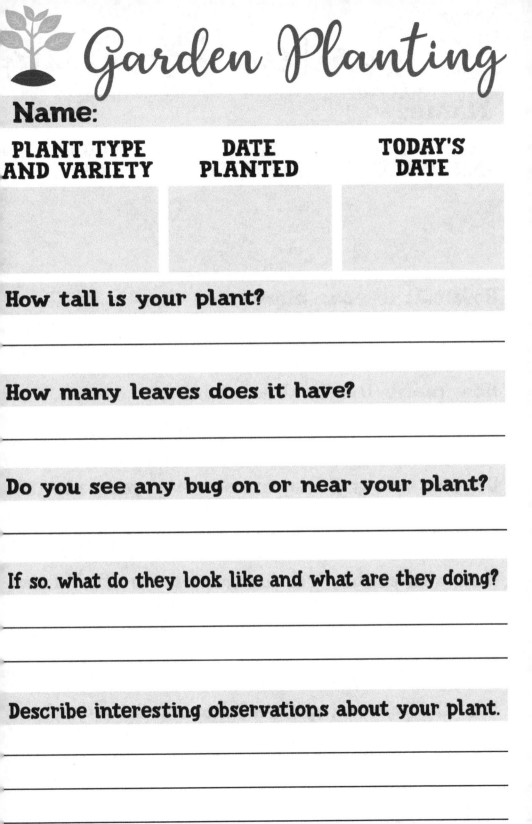

Garden Planting

Name:

PLANT TYPE AND VARIETY	DATE PLANTED	TODAY'S DATE

How tall is your plant?

_____

How many leaves does it have?

_____

Do you see any bug on or near your plant?

_____

If so. what do they look like and what are they doing?

_____

_____

Describe interesting observations about your plant.

_____

_____

_____

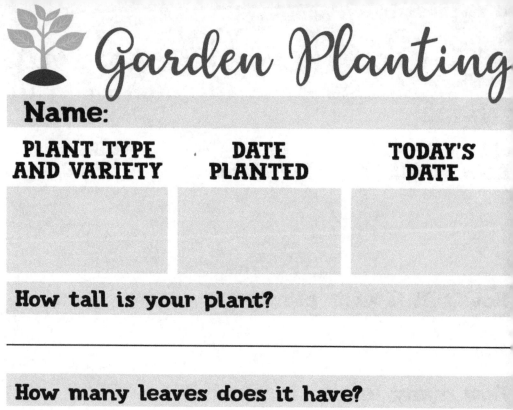

Garden Planting

Name:

PLANT TYPE AND VARIETY	DATE PLANTED	TODAY'S DATE

How tall is your plant?

_____

How many leaves does it have?

_____

Do you see any bug on or near your plant?

_____

If so. what do they look like and what are they doing?

_____

_____

Describe interesting observations about your plant.

_____

_____

_____

Garden Planting

Name:

PLANT TYPE AND VARIETY	DATE PLANTED	TODAY'S DATE

How tall is your plant?

_____

How many leaves does it have?

_____

Do you see any bug on or near your plant?

_____

If so, what do they look like and what are they doing?

_____

_____

Describe interesting observations about your plant.

_____

_____

_____

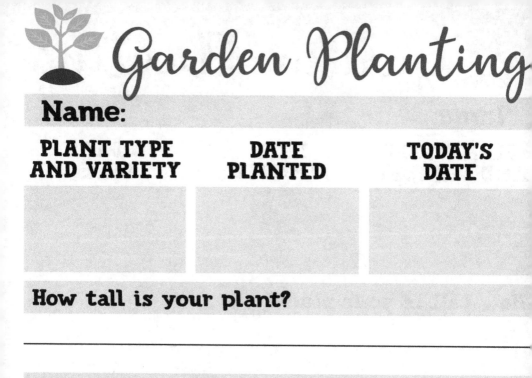

Garden Planting

Name:

PLANT TYPE AND VARIETY	DATE PLANTED	TODAY'S DATE

How tall is your plant?

_____

How many leaves does it have?

_____

Do you see any bug on or near your plant?

_____

If so, what do they look like and what are they doing?

_____

_____

Describe interesting observations about your plant.

_____

_____

_____

Garden Planting

Name:

PLANT TYPE AND VARIETY	DATE PLANTED	TODAY'S DATE

How tall is your plant?

_____

How many leaves does it have?

_____

Do you see any bug on or near your plant?

_____

If so. what do they look like and what are they doing?

_____

_____

Describe interesting observations about your plant.

_____

_____

_____

Garden Planting

Name:

PLANT TYPE AND VARIETY	DATE PLANTED	TODAY'S DATE

How tall is your plant?

_____

How many leaves does it have?

_____

Do you see any bug on or near your plant?

_____

If so, what do they look like and what are they doing?

_____

_____

Describe interesting observations about your plant.

_____

_____

_____

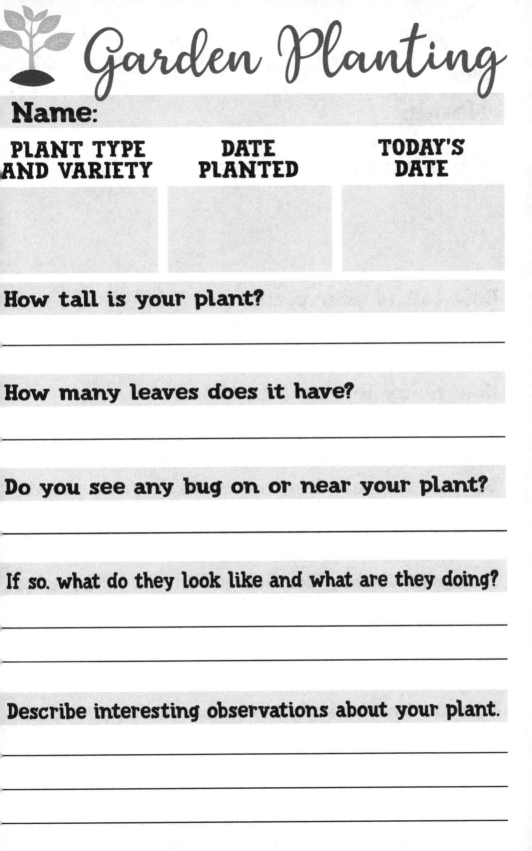

Garden Planting

Name:

PLANT TYPE AND VARIETY	DATE PLANTED	TODAY'S DATE

How tall is your plant?

_____

How many leaves does it have?

_____

Do you see any bug on or near your plant?

_____

If so. what do they look like and what are they doing?

_____

_____

Describe interesting observations about your plant.

_____

_____

_____

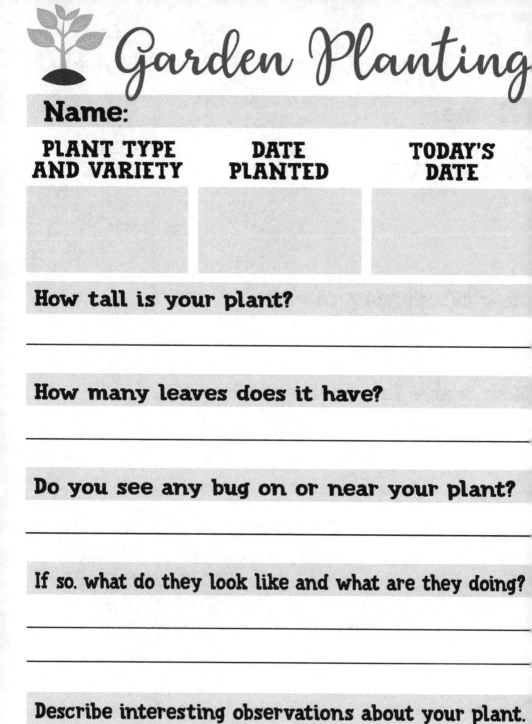

Garden Planting

Name:

PLANT TYPE AND VARIETY	DATE PLANTED	TODAY'S DATE

How tall is your plant?

_____

How many leaves does it have?

_____

Do you see any bug on or near your plant?

_____

If so, what do they look like and what are they doing?

_____

_____

Describe interesting observations about your plant.

_____

_____

_____

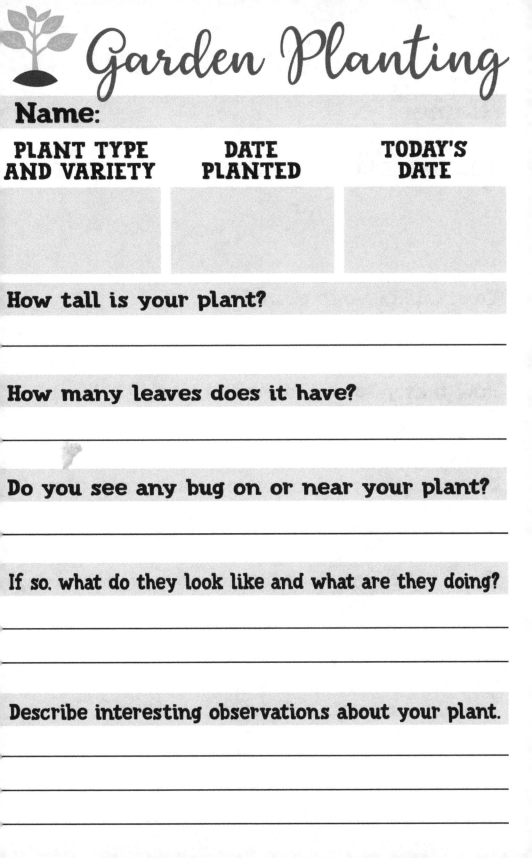

Garden Planting

Name:

PLANT TYPE AND VARIETY	DATE PLANTED	TODAY'S DATE

How tall is your plant?

_____

How many leaves does it have?

_____

Do you see any bug on or near your plant?

_____

If so, what do they look like and what are they doing?

_____

_____

Describe interesting observations about your plant.

_____

_____

_____

Garden Planting

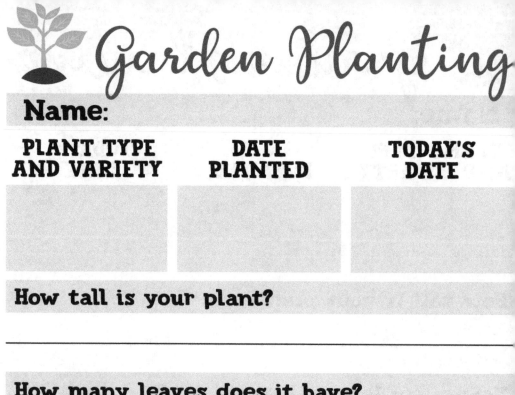

Name:

PLANT TYPE AND VARIETY	DATE PLANTED	TODAY'S DATE

How tall is your plant?

_____

How many leaves does it have?

_____

Do you see any bug on or near your plant?

_____

If so. what do they look like and what are they doing?

_____

_____

Describe interesting observations about your plant.

_____

_____

_____

Garden Planting

Name:

PLANT TYPE AND VARIETY	DATE PLANTED	TODAY'S DATE

How tall is your plant?

_____

How many leaves does it have?

_____

Do you see any bug on or near your plant?

_____

If so. what do they look like and what are they doing?

_____

_____

Describe interesting observations about your plant.

_____

_____

_____

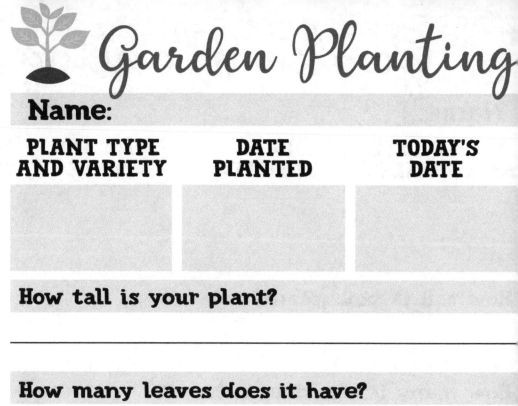

Garden Planting

Name:

PLANT TYPE AND VARIETY	DATE PLANTED	TODAY'S DATE

How tall is your plant?

_____

How many leaves does it have?

_____

Do you see any bug on or near your plant?

_____

If so, what do they look like and what are they doing?

_____

_____

Describe interesting observations about your plant.

_____

_____

_____

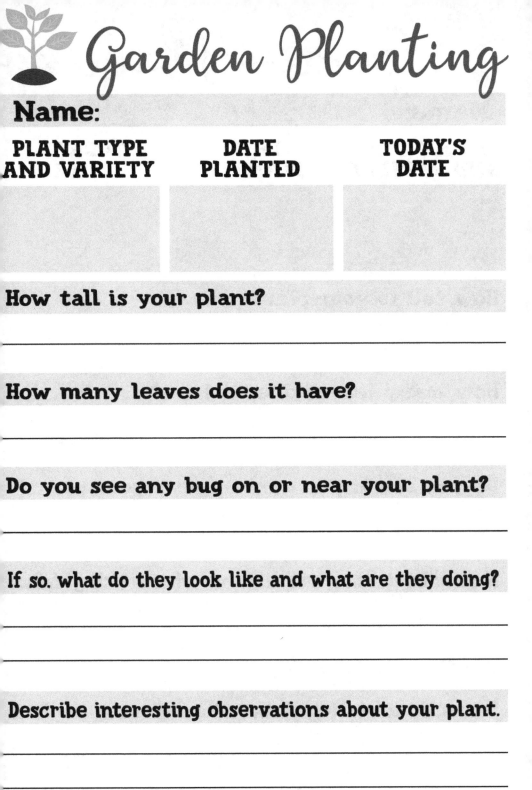

Garden Planting

Name:

PLANT TYPE AND VARIETY	DATE PLANTED	TODAY'S DATE

How tall is your plant?

_____

How many leaves does it have?

_____

Do you see any bug on or near your plant?

_____

If so. what do they look like and what are they doing?

_____

_____

Describe interesting observations about your plant.

_____

_____

_____

_____

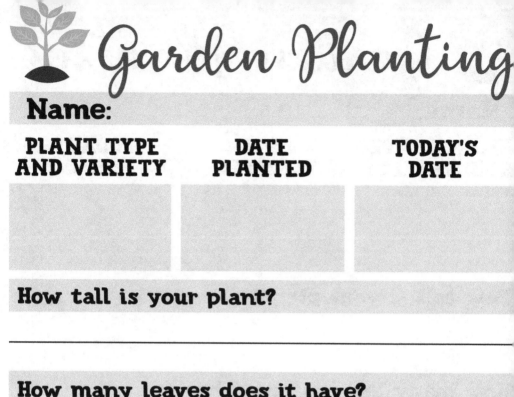

Garden Planting

Name:

PLANT TYPE AND VARIETY	DATE PLANTED	TODAY'S DATE

How tall is your plant?

_____

How many leaves does it have?

_____

Do you see any bug on or near your plant?

_____

If so, what do they look like and what are they doing?

_____

_____

Describe interesting observations about your plant.

_____

_____

_____

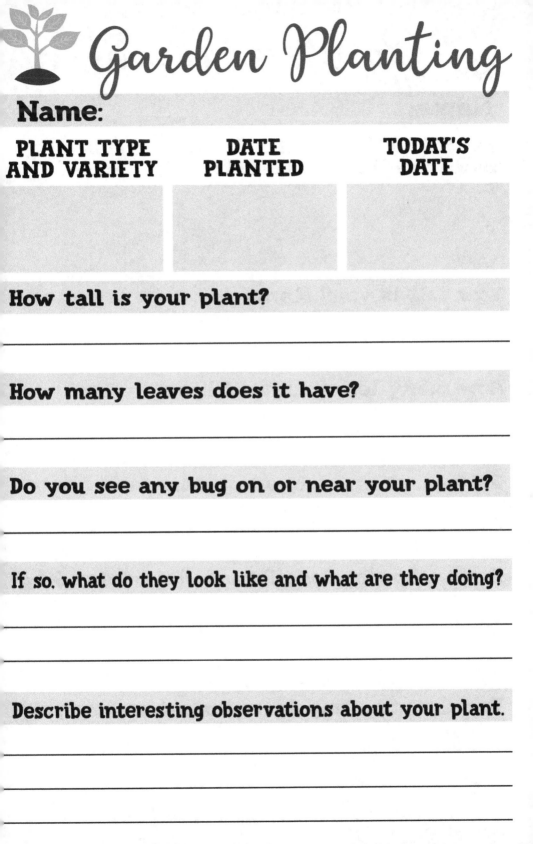

Garden Planting

Name:

PLANT TYPE AND VARIETY	DATE PLANTED	TODAY'S DATE

How tall is your plant?

_____

How many leaves does it have?

_____

Do you see any bug on or near your plant?

_____

If so, what do they look like and what are they doing?

_____

_____

Describe interesting observations about your plant.

_____

_____

_____

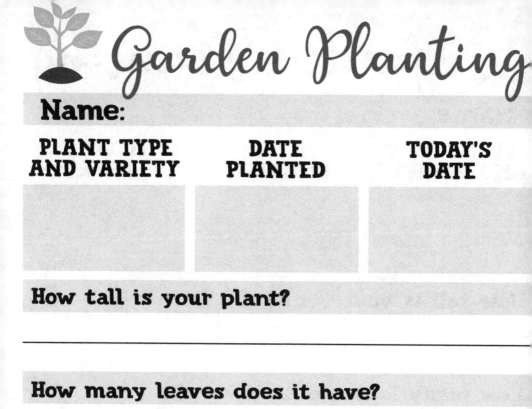

Garden Planting

Name:

PLANT TYPE AND VARIETY	DATE PLANTED	TODAY'S DATE

How tall is your plant?

_____

How many leaves does it have?

_____

Do you see any bug on or near your plant?

_____

If so, what do they look like and what are they doing?

_____

_____

Describe interesting observations about your plant.

_____

_____

_____

Garden Planting

Name:

PLANT TYPE AND VARIETY	DATE PLANTED	TODAY'S DATE

How tall is your plant?

_____

How many leaves does it have?

_____

Do you see any bug on or near your plant?

_____

If so. what do they look like and what are they doing?

_____

_____

Describe interesting observations about your plant.

_____

_____

_____

_____

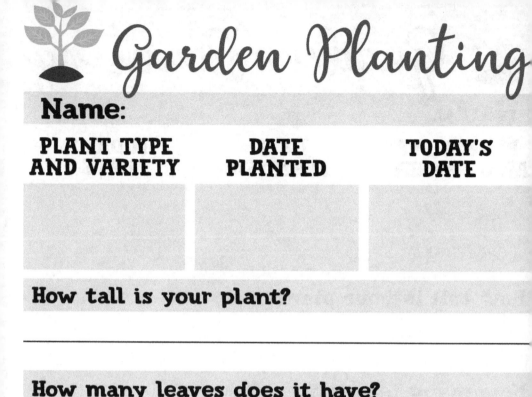

Garden Planting

Name:

PLANT TYPE AND VARIETY	DATE PLANTED	TODAY'S DATE

How tall is your plant?

_____

How many leaves does it have?

_____

Do you see any bug on or near your plant?

_____

If so, what do they look like and what are they doing?

_____

_____

Describe interesting observations about your plant.

_____

_____

_____

Garden Planting

Name:

PLANT TYPE AND VARIETY	DATE PLANTED	TODAY'S DATE

How tall is your plant?

_____

How many leaves does it have?

_____

Do you see any bug on or near your plant?

_____

If so. what do they look like and what are they doing?

_____

_____

Describe interesting observations about your plant.

_____

_____

_____

Garden Planting

Name:

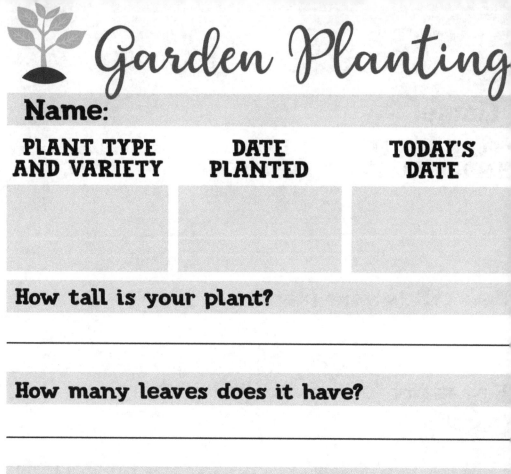

PLANT TYPE AND VARIETY	DATE PLANTED	TODAY'S DATE

How tall is your plant?

_____

How many leaves does it have?

_____

Do you see any bug on or near your plant?

_____

If so, what do they look like and what are they doing?

_____

_____

Describe interesting observations about your plant.

_____

_____

_____

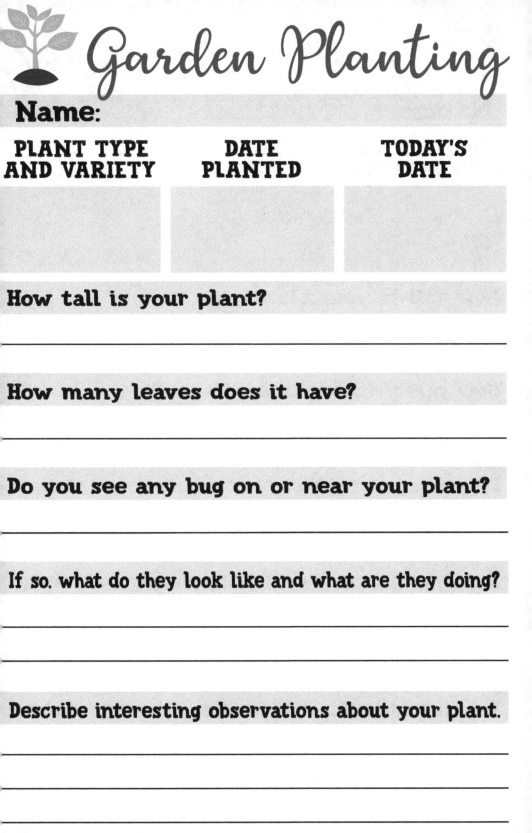

Garden Planting

Name:

PLANT TYPE AND VARIETY	DATE PLANTED	TODAY'S DATE

How tall is your plant?

_____

How many leaves does it have?

_____

Do you see any bug on or near your plant?

_____

If so. what do they look like and what are they doing?

_____
_____

Describe interesting observations about your plant.

_____
_____
_____

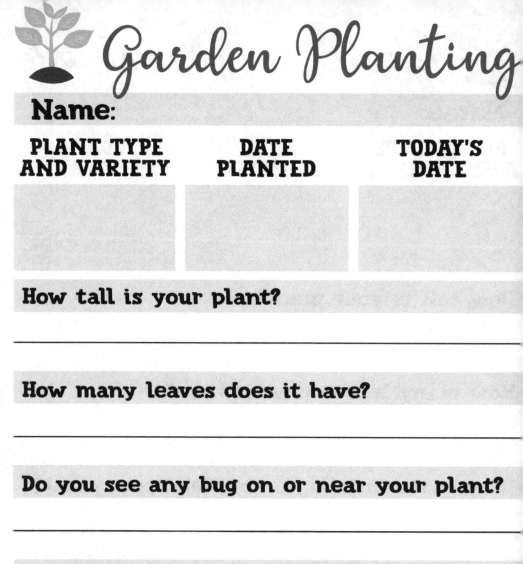

Garden Planting

Name:

PLANT TYPE AND VARIETY	DATE PLANTED	TODAY'S DATE

How tall is your plant?

_____

How many leaves does it have?

_____

Do you see any bug on or near your plant?

_____

If so, what do they look like and what are they doing?

_____

_____

Describe interesting observations about your plant.

_____

_____

_____

Garden Planting

Name:

PLANT TYPE AND VARIETY	DATE PLANTED	TODAY'S DATE

How tall is your plant?

_____

How many leaves does it have?

_____

Do you see any bug on or near your plant?

_____

If so. what do they look like and what are they doing?

_____

_____

Describe interesting observations about your plant.

_____

_____

_____

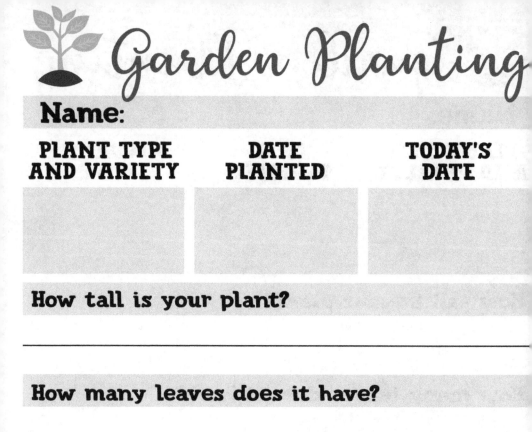

Garden Planting

Name:

PLANT TYPE AND VARIETY	DATE PLANTED	TODAY'S DATE

How tall is your plant?

_____

How many leaves does it have?

_____

Do you see any bug on or near your plant?

_____

If so. what do they look like and what are they doing?

_____

_____

Describe interesting observations about your plant.

_____

_____

_____

Garden Planting

Name:

PLANT TYPE AND VARIETY	DATE PLANTED	TODAY'S DATE

How tall is your plant?

_____

How many leaves does it have?

_____

Do you see any bug on or near your plant?

_____

If so. what do they look like and what are they doing?

_____

_____

Describe interesting observations about your plant.

_____

_____

_____

_____

Garden Planting

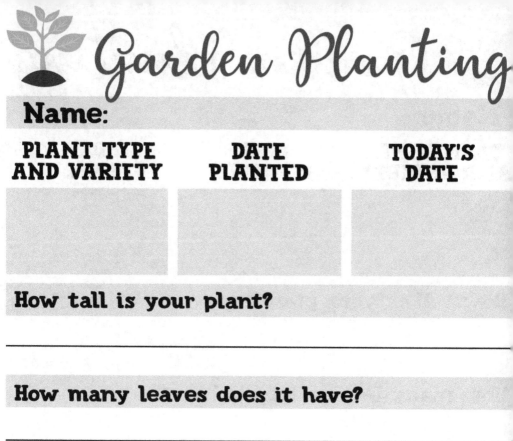

Name:

PLANT TYPE AND VARIETY	DATE PLANTED	TODAY'S DATE

How tall is your plant?

_____

How many leaves does it have?

_____

Do you see any bug on or near your plant?

_____

If so, what do they look like and what are they doing?

_____

_____

Describe interesting observations about your plant.

_____

_____

_____

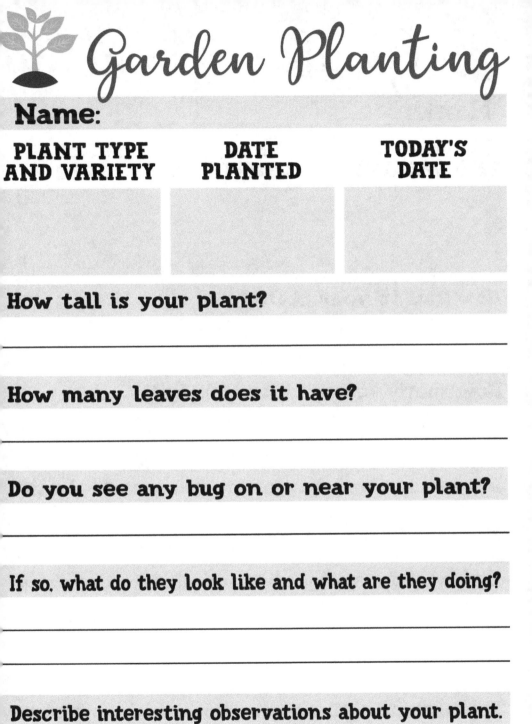

Garden Planting

Name:

PLANT TYPE AND VARIETY	DATE PLANTED	TODAY'S DATE

How tall is your plant?

_____

How many leaves does it have?

_____

Do you see any bug on or near your plant?

_____

If so, what do they look like and what are they doing?

_____

_____

Describe interesting observations about your plant.

_____

_____

_____

_____

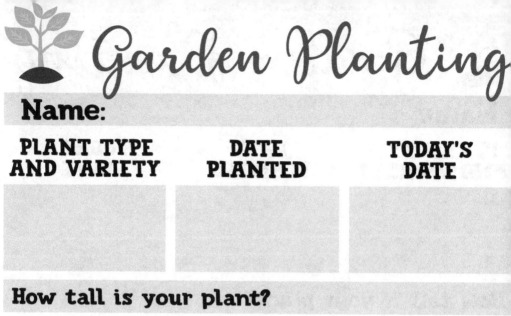

Garden Planting

Name:

PLANT TYPE AND VARIETY	DATE PLANTED	TODAY'S DATE

How tall is your plant?

_____

How many leaves does it have?

_____

Do you see any bug on or near your plant?

_____

If so. what do they look like and what are they doing?

_____

_____

Describe interesting observations about your plant.

_____

_____

_____

Garden Planting

Name:

PLANT TYPE AND VARIETY	DATE PLANTED	TODAY'S DATE

How tall is your plant?

_____

How many leaves does it have?

_____

Do you see any bug on or near your plant?

_____

If so. what do they look like and what are they doing?

_____

_____

Describe interesting observations about your plant.

_____

_____

_____

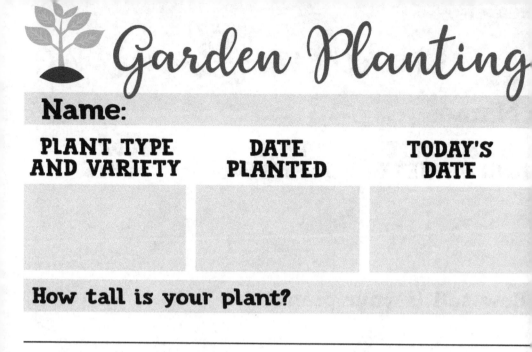

Garden Planting

Name:

PLANT TYPE AND VARIETY	DATE PLANTED	TODAY'S DATE

How tall is your plant?

_____

How many leaves does it have?

_____

Do you see any bug on or near your plant?

_____

If so. what do they look like and what are they doing?

_____

_____

Describe interesting observations about your plant.

_____

_____

_____

Garden Planting

Name:

PLANT TYPE AND VARIETY	DATE PLANTED	TODAY'S DATE

How tall is your plant?

_____

How many leaves does it have?

_____

Do you see any bug on or near your plant?

_____

If so. what do they look like and what are they doing?

_____

_____

Describe interesting observations about your plant.

_____

_____

_____

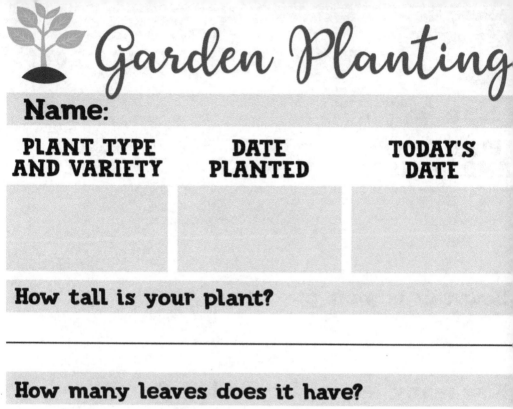

Garden Planting

Name:

PLANT TYPE AND VARIETY	DATE PLANTED	TODAY'S DATE

How tall is your plant?

_____

How many leaves does it have?

_____

Do you see any bug on or near your plant?

_____

If so, what do they look like and what are they doing?

_____

_____

Describe interesting observations about your plant.

_____

_____

_____

Garden Planting

Name:

PLANT TYPE AND VARIETY	DATE PLANTED	TODAY'S DATE

How tall is your plant?

_____

How many leaves does it have?

_____

Do you see any bug on or near your plant?

_____

If so, what do they look like and what are they doing?

_____

_____

Describe interesting observations about your plant.

_____

_____

_____

Garden Planting

Name:

PLANT TYPE AND VARIETY	DATE PLANTED	TODAY'S DATE

How tall is your plant?

_____

How many leaves does it have?

_____

Do you see any bug on or near your plant?

_____

If so. what do they look like and what are they doing?

_____

_____

Describe interesting observations about your plant.

_____

_____

_____

Garden Planting

Name:

PLANT TYPE AND VARIETY	DATE PLANTED	TODAY'S DATE

How tall is your plant?

_____

How many leaves does it have?

_____

Do you see any bug on or near your plant?

_____

If so. what do they look like and what are they doing?

_____

_____

Describe interesting observations about your plant.

_____

_____

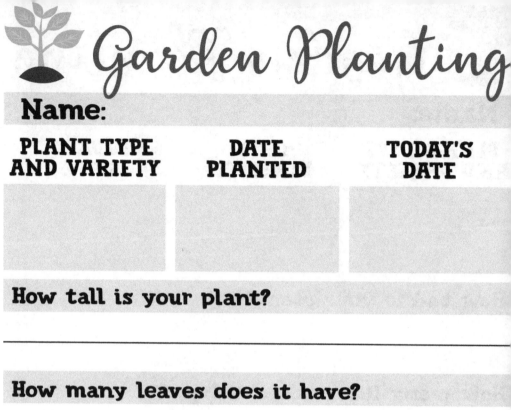

Garden Planting

Name:

PLANT TYPE AND VARIETY	DATE PLANTED	TODAY'S DATE

How tall is your plant?

_____

How many leaves does it have?

_____

Do you see any bug on or near your plant?

_____

If so. what do they look like and what are they doing?

_____

_____

Describe interesting observations about your plant.

_____

_____

_____

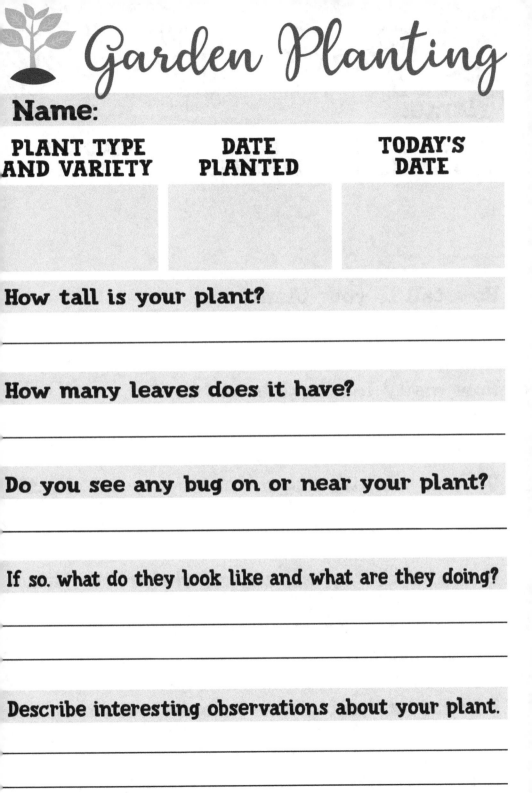

Garden Planting

Name:

PLANT TYPE AND VARIETY	DATE PLANTED	TODAY'S DATE

How tall is your plant?

_____

How many leaves does it have?

_____

Do you see any bug on or near your plant?

_____

If so. what do they look like and what are they doing?

_____

_____

Describe interesting observations about your plant.

_____

_____

_____

Garden Planting

Name:

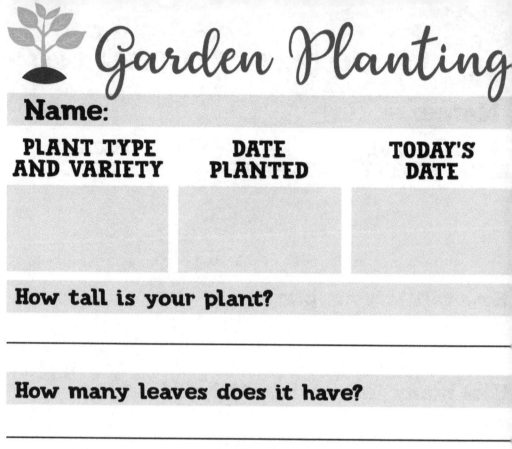

PLANT TYPE AND VARIETY	DATE PLANTED	TODAY'S DATE

How tall is your plant?

_____

How many leaves does it have?

_____

Do you see any bug on or near your plant?

_____

If so. what do they look like and what are they doing?

_____

_____

Describe interesting observations about your plant.

_____

_____

_____

Garden Planting

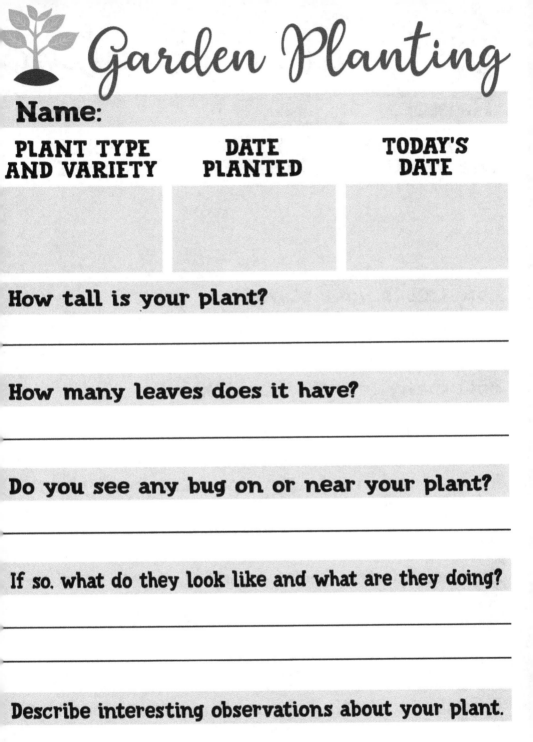

Name:

PLANT TYPE AND VARIETY	DATE PLANTED	TODAY'S DATE

How tall is your plant?

_____

How many leaves does it have?

_____

Do you see any bug on or near your plant?

_____

If so, what do they look like and what are they doing?

_____

_____

Describe interesting observations about your plant.

_____

_____

_____

_____

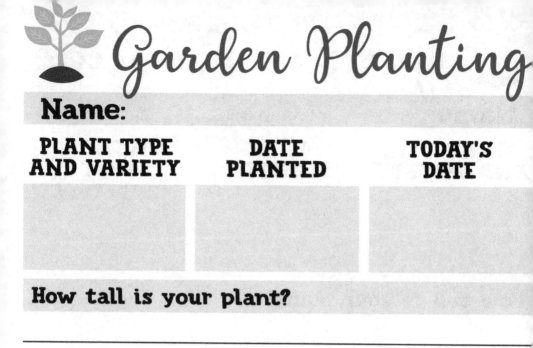

Garden Planting

Name:

PLANT TYPE AND VARIETY	DATE PLANTED	TODAY'S DATE

How tall is your plant?

_____

How many leaves does it have?

_____

Do you see any bug on or near your plant?

_____

If so, what do they look like and what are they doing?

_____

_____

Describe interesting observations about your plant.

_____

_____

_____

Garden Planting

Name:

PLANT TYPE AND VARIETY	DATE PLANTED	TODAY'S DATE

How tall is your plant?

_____

How many leaves does it have?

_____

Do you see any bug on or near your plant?

_____

If so. what do they look like and what are they doing?

_____

_____

Describe interesting observations about your plant.

_____

_____

_____

Garden Planting

Name:

PLANT TYPE AND VARIETY	DATE PLANTED	TODAY'S DATE

How tall is your plant?

_____

How many leaves does it have?

_____

Do you see any bug on or near your plant?

_____

If so. what do they look like and what are they doing?

_____

_____

Describe interesting observations about your plant.

_____

_____

_____

Garden Planting

Name:

PLANT TYPE AND VARIETY	DATE PLANTED	TODAY'S DATE

How tall is your plant?

_____

How many leaves does it have?

_____

Do you see any bug on or near your plant?

_____

If so. what do they look like and what are they doing?

_____

_____

Describe interesting observations about your plant.

_____

_____

_____

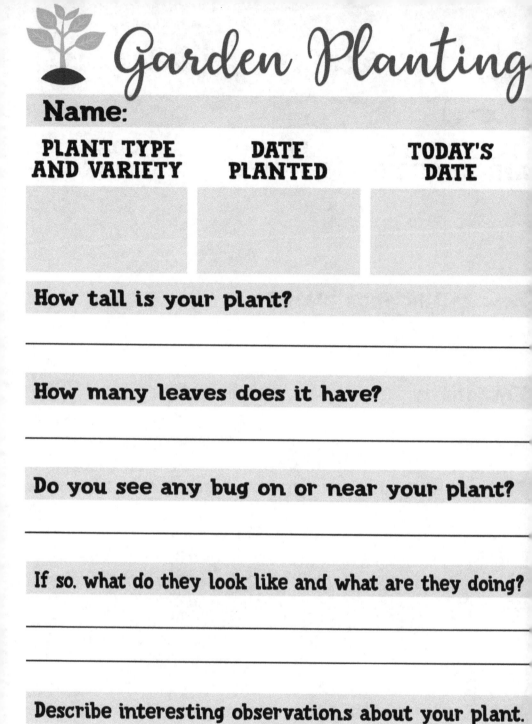

Garden Planting

Name:

PLANT TYPE AND VARIETY	DATE PLANTED	TODAY'S DATE

How tall is your plant?

_____

How many leaves does it have?

_____

Do you see any bug on or near your plant?

_____

If so, what do they look like and what are they doing?

_____

_____

Describe interesting observations about your plant.

_____

_____

_____

Garden Planting

Name:

PLANT TYPE AND VARIETY	DATE PLANTED	TODAY'S DATE

How tall is your plant?

_____

How many leaves does it have?

_____

Do you see any bug on or near your plant?

_____

If so, what do they look like and what are they doing?

_____

_____

Describe interesting observations about your plant.

_____

_____

_____

Garden Planting

Name:

PLANT TYPE AND VARIETY	DATE PLANTED	TODAY'S DATE

How tall is your plant?

_____

How many leaves does it have?

_____

Do you see any bug on or near your plant?

_____

If so, what do they look like and what are they doing?

_____

_____

Describe interesting observations about your plant.

_____

_____

_____

Garden Planting

Name:

PLANT TYPE AND VARIETY	DATE PLANTED	TODAY'S DATE

How tall is your plant?

_____

How many leaves does it have?

_____

Do you see any bug on or near your plant?

_____

If so. what do they look like and what are they doing?

_____

_____

Describe interesting observations about your plant.

_____

_____

_____

Garden Planting

Name:

PLANT TYPE AND VARIETY	DATE PLANTED	TODAY'S DATE

How tall is your plant?

How many leaves does it have?

Do you see any bug on or near your plant?

If so, what do they look like and what are they doing?

Describe interesting observations about your plant.

Garden Planting

Name:

PLANT TYPE AND VARIETY	DATE PLANTED	TODAY'S DATE

How tall is your plant?

_____

How many leaves does it have?

_____

Do you see any bug on or near your plant?

_____

If so. what do they look like and what are they doing?

_____

_____

Describe interesting observations about your plant.

_____

_____

_____

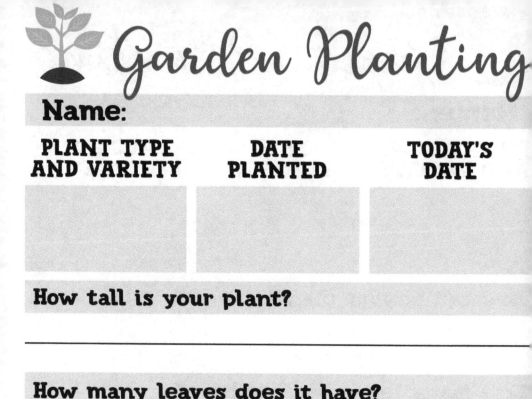

Garden Planting

Name:

PLANT TYPE AND VARIETY	DATE PLANTED	TODAY'S DATE

How tall is your plant?

_____

How many leaves does it have?

_____

Do you see any bug on or near your plant?

_____

If so, what do they look like and what are they doing?

_____

_____

Describe interesting observations about your plant.

_____

_____

_____

Garden Planting

Name:

PLANT TYPE AND VARIETY	DATE PLANTED	TODAY'S DATE

How tall is your plant?

_____

How many leaves does it have?

_____

Do you see any bug on or near your plant?

_____

If so. what do they look like and what are they doing?

_____

_____

Describe interesting observations about your plant.

_____

_____

_____

Garden Planting

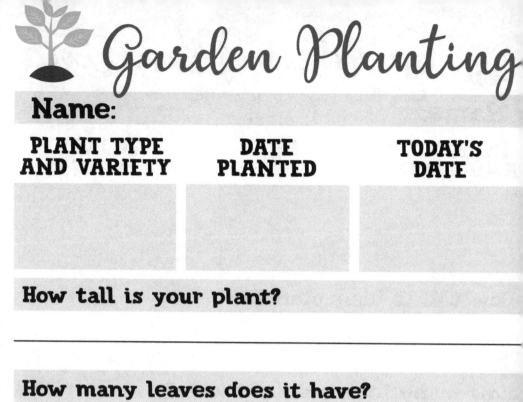

Name:

PLANT TYPE AND VARIETY	DATE PLANTED	TODAY'S DATE

How tall is your plant?

_____

How many leaves does it have?

_____

Do you see any bug on or near your plant?

_____

If so. what do they look like and what are they doing?

_____

_____

Describe interesting observations about your plant.

_____

_____

_____

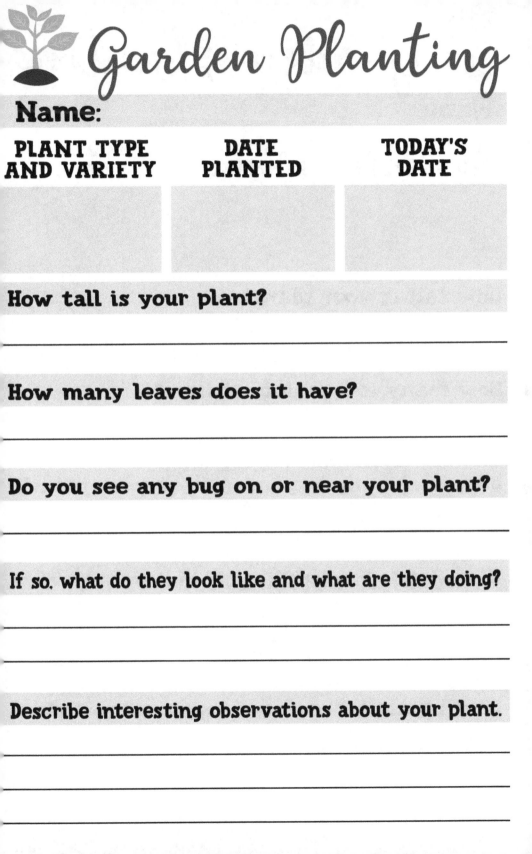

Garden Planting

Name:

PLANT TYPE AND VARIETY	DATE PLANTED	TODAY'S DATE

How tall is your plant?

_____

How many leaves does it have?

_____

Do you see any bug on or near your plant?

_____

If so. what do they look like and what are they doing?

_____

_____

Describe interesting observations about your plant.

_____

_____

_____

_____

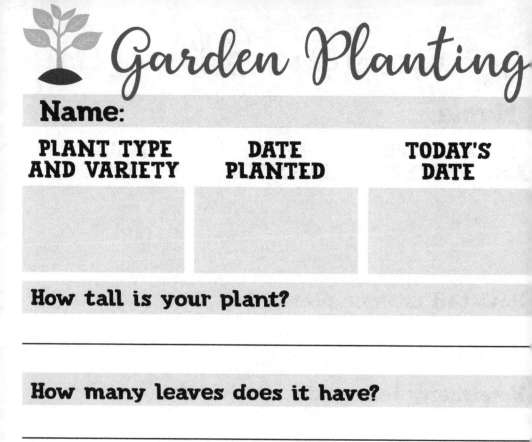

Garden Planting

Name:

PLANT TYPE AND VARIETY	DATE PLANTED	TODAY'S DATE

How tall is your plant?

_____

How many leaves does it have?

_____

Do you see any bug on or near your plant?

_____

If so. what do they look like and what are they doing?

_____

_____

Describe interesting observations about your plant.

_____

_____

_____

Garden Planting

Name:

PLANT TYPE AND VARIETY	DATE PLANTED	TODAY'S DATE

How tall is your plant?

_____

How many leaves does it have?

_____

Do you see any bug on or near your plant?

_____

If so. what do they look like and what are they doing?

_____

_____

Describe interesting observations about your plant.

_____

_____

_____

Garden Planting

Name:

PLANT TYPE AND VARIETY	DATE PLANTED	TODAY'S DATE

How tall is your plant?

_____

How many leaves does it have?

_____

Do you see any bug on or near your plant?

_____

If so, what do they look like and what are they doing?

_____

_____

Describe interesting observations about your plant.

_____

_____

_____

Garden Planting

Name:

PLANT TYPE AND VARIETY	DATE PLANTED	TODAY'S DATE

How tall is your plant?

_____

How many leaves does it have?

_____

Do you see any bug on or near your plant?

_____

If so, what do they look like and what are they doing?

_____

_____

Describe interesting observations about your plant.

_____

_____

_____

Garden Planting

Name:

PLANT TYPE AND VARIETY	DATE PLANTED	TODAY'S DATE

How tall is your plant?

_____

How many leaves does it have?

_____

Do you see any bug on or near your plant?

_____

If so. what do they look like and what are they doing?

_____

_____

Describe interesting observations about your plant.

_____

_____

_____

Garden Planting

Name:

PLANT TYPE AND VARIETY	DATE PLANTED	TODAY'S DATE

How tall is your plant?

_____

How many leaves does it have?

_____

Do you see any bug on or near your plant?

_____

If so. what do they look like and what are they doing?

_____

_____

Describe interesting observations about your plant.

_____

_____

_____

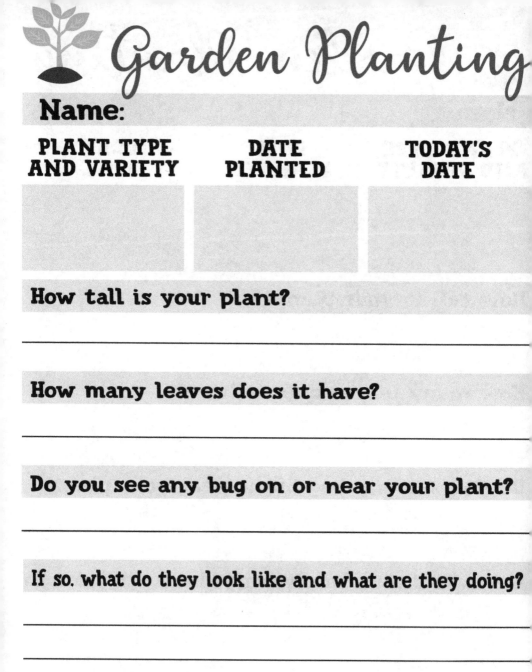

Garden Planting

Name:

PLANT TYPE AND VARIETY	DATE PLANTED	TODAY'S DATE

How tall is your plant?

_____

How many leaves does it have?

_____

Do you see any bug on or near your plant?

_____

If so. what do they look like and what are they doing?

_____

_____

Describe interesting observations about your plant.

_____

_____

_____

Garden Planting

Name:

PLANT TYPE AND VARIETY	DATE PLANTED	TODAY'S DATE

How tall is your plant?

_____

How many leaves does it have?

_____

Do you see any bug on or near your plant?

_____

If so. what do they look like and what are they doing?

_____

_____

Describe interesting observations about your plant.

_____

_____

_____

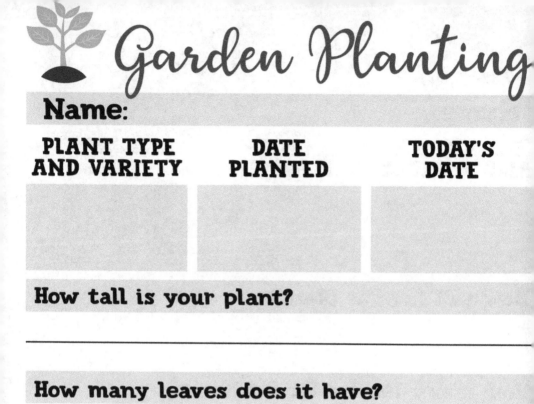

Garden Planting

Name:

PLANT TYPE AND VARIETY	DATE PLANTED	TODAY'S DATE

How tall is your plant?

_____

How many leaves does it have?

_____

Do you see any bug on or near your plant?

_____

If so. what do they look like and what are they doing?

_____

_____

Describe interesting observations about your plant.

_____

_____

_____

Garden Planting

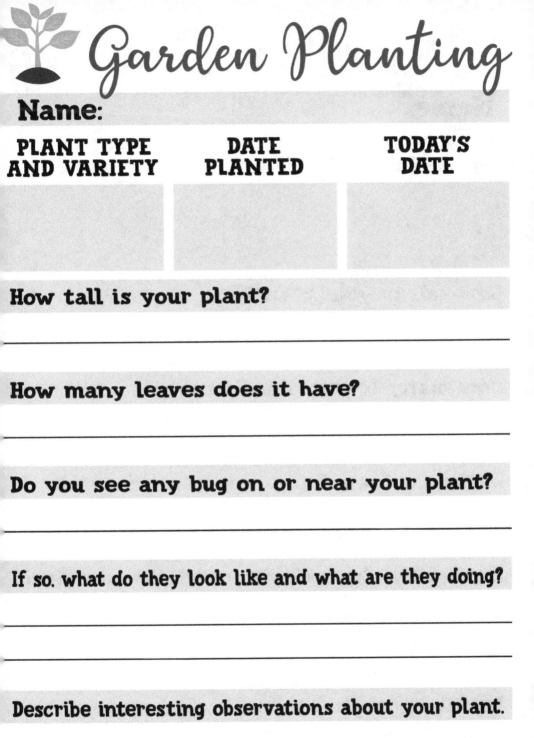

Name:

PLANT TYPE AND VARIETY	DATE PLANTED	TODAY'S DATE

How tall is your plant?

_____

How many leaves does it have?

_____

Do you see any bug on or near your plant?

_____

If so. what do they look like and what are they doing?

_____

_____

Describe interesting observations about your plant.

_____

_____

_____

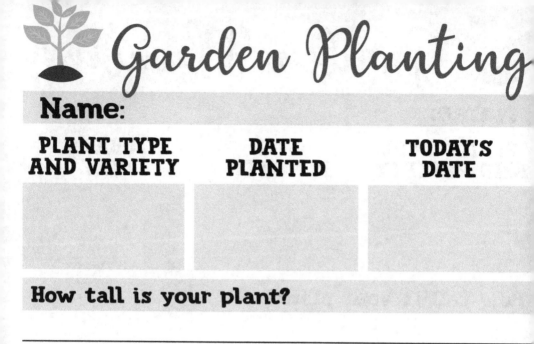

Garden Planting

Name:

PLANT TYPE AND VARIETY	DATE PLANTED	TODAY'S DATE

How tall is your plant?

_____

How many leaves does it have?

_____

Do you see any bug on or near your plant?

_____

If so. what do they look like and what are they doing?

_____

_____

Describe interesting observations about your plant.

_____

_____

_____

Garden Planting

Name:

PLANT TYPE AND VARIETY	DATE PLANTED	TODAY'S DATE

How tall is your plant?

_____

How many leaves does it have?

_____

Do you see any bug on or near your plant?

_____

If so. what do they look like and what are they doing?

_____

_____

Describe interesting observations about your plant.

_____

_____

_____

Garden Planting

Name:

PLANT TYPE AND VARIETY	DATE PLANTED	TODAY'S DATE

How tall is your plant?

_____

How many leaves does it have?

_____

Do you see any bug on or near your plant?

_____

If so. what do they look like and what are they doing?

_____

_____

Describe interesting observations about your plant.

_____

_____

_____

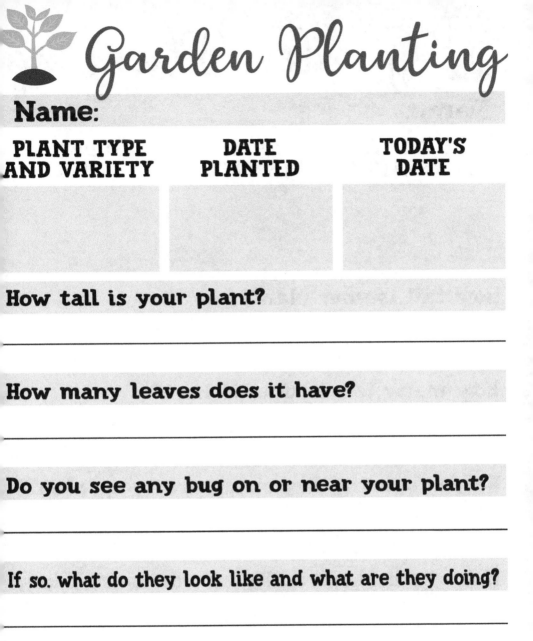

Garden Planting

Name:

PLANT TYPE AND VARIETY	DATE PLANTED	TODAY'S DATE

How tall is your plant?

_____

How many leaves does it have?

_____

Do you see any bug on or near your plant?

_____

If so. what do they look like and what are they doing?

_____

_____

Describe interesting observations about your plant.

_____

_____

_____

Garden Planting

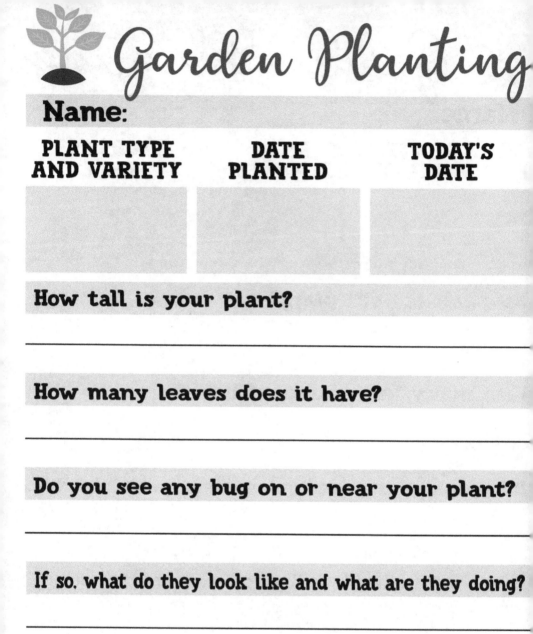

Name:

PLANT TYPE AND VARIETY	DATE PLANTED	TODAY'S DATE

How tall is your plant?

_____

How many leaves does it have?

_____

Do you see any bug on or near your plant?

_____

If so, what do they look like and what are they doing?

_____

_____

Describe interesting observations about your plant.

_____

_____

_____

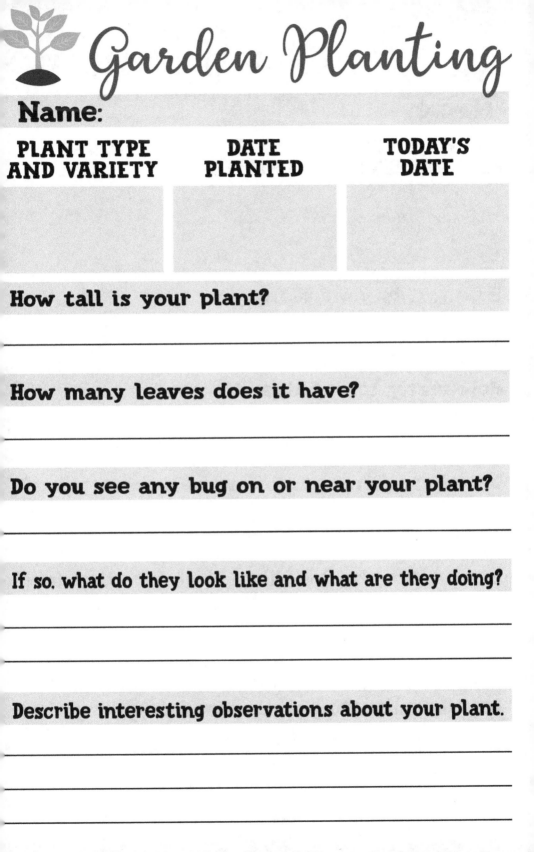

Garden Planting

Name:

PLANT TYPE AND VARIETY	DATE PLANTED	TODAY'S DATE

How tall is your plant?

How many leaves does it have?

Do you see any bug on or near your plant?

If so. what do they look like and what are they doing?

Describe interesting observations about your plant.

Garden Planting

Name:

PLANT TYPE AND VARIETY	DATE PLANTED	TODAY'S DATE

How tall is your plant?

_____

How many leaves does it have?

_____

Do you see any bug on or near your plant?

_____

If so. what do they look like and what are they doing?

_____

_____

Describe interesting observations about your plant.

_____

_____

_____

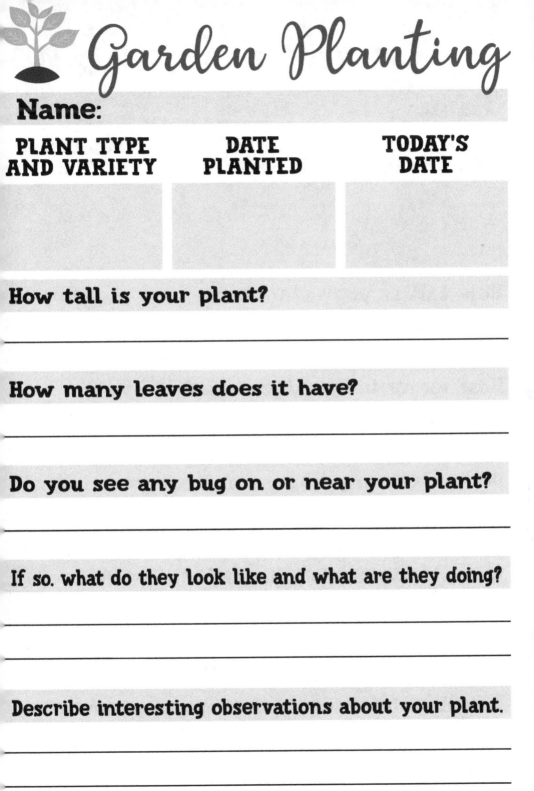

Garden Planting

Name:

PLANT TYPE AND VARIETY	DATE PLANTED	TODAY'S DATE

How tall is your plant?

_____

How many leaves does it have?

_____

Do you see any bug on or near your plant?

_____

If so. what do they look like and what are they doing?

_____

_____

Describe interesting observations about your plant.

_____

_____

_____

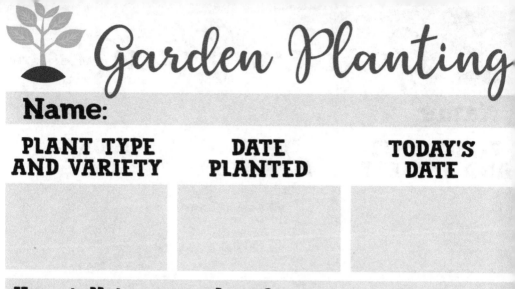

Garden Planting

Name:

PLANT TYPE AND VARIETY	DATE PLANTED	TODAY'S DATE

How tall is your plant?

_____

How many leaves does it have?

_____

Do you see any bug on or near your plant?

_____

If so, what do they look like and what are they doing?

_____

_____

Describe interesting observations about your plant.

_____

_____

_____

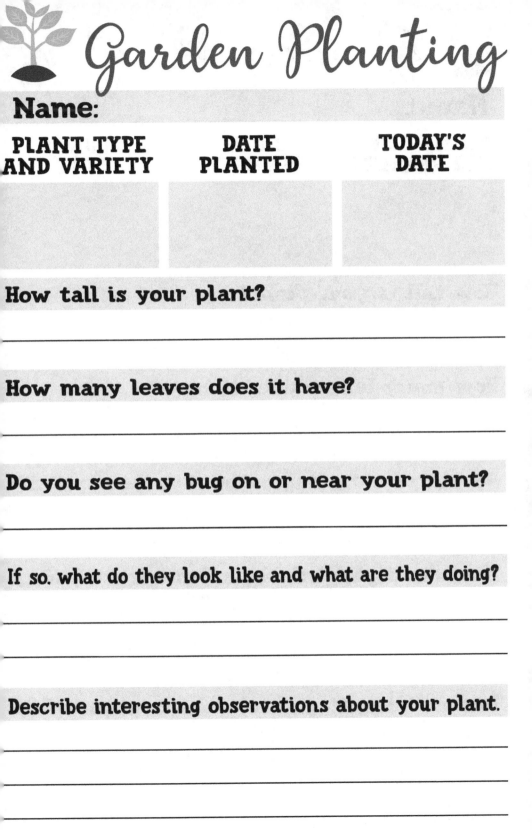

Garden Planting

Name:

PLANT TYPE AND VARIETY	DATE PLANTED	TODAY'S DATE

How tall is your plant?

_____

How many leaves does it have?

_____

Do you see any bug on or near your plant?

_____

If so. what do they look like and what are they doing?

_____

_____

Describe interesting observations about your plant.

_____

_____

_____

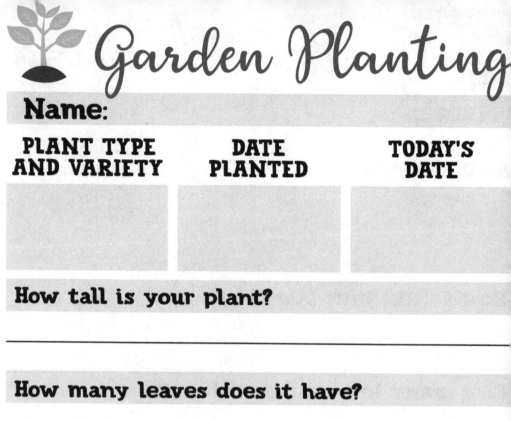

Garden Planting

Name:

PLANT TYPE AND VARIETY	DATE PLANTED	TODAY'S DATE

How tall is your plant?

_____

How many leaves does it have?

_____

Do you see any bug on or near your plant?

_____

If so, what do they look like and what are they doing?

_____

_____

Describe interesting observations about your plant.

_____

_____

_____

Garden Planting

Name:

PLANT TYPE AND VARIETY	DATE PLANTED	TODAY'S DATE

How tall is your plant?

_____

How many leaves does it have?

_____

Do you see any bug on or near your plant?

_____

If so. what do they look like and what are they doing?

_____

_____

Describe interesting observations about your plant.

_____

_____

_____

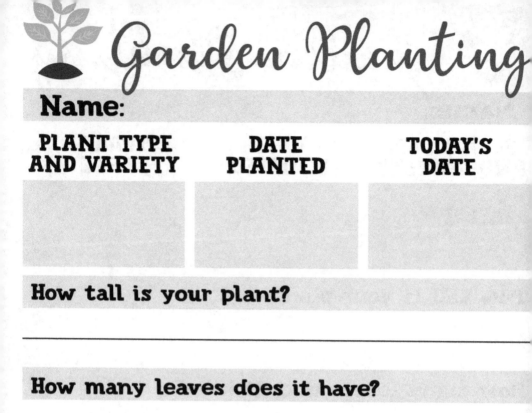

Garden Planting

Name:

PLANT TYPE AND VARIETY	DATE PLANTED	TODAY'S DATE

How tall is your plant?

_____

How many leaves does it have?

_____

Do you see any bug on or near your plant?

_____

If so. what do they look like and what are they doing?

_____

_____

Describe interesting observations about your plant.

_____

_____

_____

CPSIA information can be obtained
at www.ICGtesting.com
Printed in the USA
LVHW080145010421
683089LV00010B/137